# Tiger's Heart

Jay Hoster

# Tiger's Heart

What Really Happened
in the *Groat's-worth of Wit*
Controversy of 1592

Ravine Books
Columbus

*Published by*
Ravine Books
1047 Birchmont Road
Columbus, Ohio 43220

Library of Congress Catalog Card Number: 93-92606

*First Printing, 1993*

Hollywood is no longer a place, it's a condition.

—SHEILAH GRAHAM

The trouble with Bogart is that he thinks he is Bogart.

—DAVE CHASEN

In the writer section, we learn of the frustrations of being a scribe in a town where everyone thinks he can write.

—A REVIEWER OF *NAKED HOLLYWOOD*,
A BBC DOCUMENTARY

Zanuck would spot a tiger the first two bites.

—A FRIEND OF DARRYL ZANUCK

When I saw David Selznick at Charlie's funeral [Charles MacArthur, screenwriter and playwright] I couldn't help but think of David's toothmarks in Charlie's arm that he still bore there in that casket.

—NUNNALLY JOHNSON

## *A Note on the Spelling of Elizabethan Words*

*Writing a book directed at specialists as well as general readers necessarily involves making some choices about the presentation of Elizabethan texts. It was clear to me that any quotation used as evidence regarding Greene's intentions in* Groat's-worth *should be presented in the original spelling. Whenever a word could be subject to confusion I have provided a gloss in brackets. While I have modernized the titles of books and plays, readers should be aware that many of the commentators that I cite have not done so. I have generally chosen to modernize quotations from Shakespeare, and for the sake of readability I have occasionally modernized other Elizabethan passages.*

# 1

ROBERT GREENE, A PROLIFIC WRITER OF PROFLIGATE WAYS, a true Elizabethan (he was born in 1558, the year that Elizabeth came to the throne), as celebrated for the excesses of his personal life as for the popularity of his prose romances, author of poems, plays, and accounts of London's criminal element, wrote nothing that has been more closely scrutinized than a passage addressed to three of his fellow playwrights and published posthumously in a 1592 book entitled *Greene's Groat's-worth of Wit.*

In a slashing attack on an egotistical and predatory actor, Greene employed a familiar image from Aesop—the crow who strutted around in peacock feathers—and hurled one of the player's celebrated lines back at him. Greene was busily sounding the tocsin, warning his colleagues of the actor's most recent—and most outrageous—claim: "Yes trust them [actors] not: for there is an vpstart Crow, beautified with our feathers, that with his *Tygers hart wrapt in a Players hyde,* supposes he is as well able to bombast out a blanke verse as the best of you: and beeing an absolute *Iohannes fac totum,* is in his owne conceit the onely Shake-scene in a countrey."

(It's worth noting that the capital *s* of "shake-scene" was in line with Elizabethan typesetters' treatment of nouns. Proper names in this text were placed in the equivalent of italics; through six early editions of *Groat's-worth* the "shake" of "shake-scene" was never highlighted in that manner. Elizabethans often used *u* and *v* interchangeably and generally wrote *i* for *j*.)

Books become old, and as they do so they go unread. That was the fate of *Groat's-worth*, which was a forgotten volume by 1778 when a scholar named Thomas Tyrwhitt announced his discovery of this passage, placing upon it an interpretation that has lasted. "There can be no doubt, I think," he commented, "that *Shake-scene* alludes to *Shakespeare*" (emphasis supplied by Tyrwhitt); and he also observed that the line serving as the source of the "tiger's heart" remark can be found in *3 Henry VI*. (It's important to keep in mind that the *Henry VI* plays have been the subject of a longstanding debate over their authorship.)

Tyrwhitt's commentary has had the effect of intertwining *Groat's-worth* with Shakespeare biography. It has all seemed so obvious—an actor who supposes he can write, a seemingly clear-cut literary allusion, that word "shake-scene." To be sure, generations of Shakespeareans have grown old trying to explain why Greene was so angry at Shakespeare; yet even as the puzzlements have mounted, there is one question that goes unconsidered: how do the scholars *know* what they *think* they know?

If you consult the authoritative *Oxford English Dictionary*, you'll be informed that "shake-scene" is "of uncertain or vague meaning"; and if that produces some significant doubt about the identification of Shakespeare as the upstart crow—something along the lines of, *if the meaning of the word is uncertain, how can there be such absolute certainty about its referent?*—then you'll have difficulty joining the ranks of the orthodox *Groat's-worth* explicators. Here, for example, is what an eminent commentator has written on the attack: "The passage is ambiguous, but there can be no doubt that 'Shake-scene' is a punning reference to Shakespeare." For the Shakespeareans the *no doubt* always trumps the *ambiguous*: they simply know that "shake-scene" refers to Shakespeare.

It's worth remembering, however, that words from another century can prove to be slippery entities in their meanings. At odd moments during the Sunday mornings of my youth I would find myself pondering the fate of slow people, who seemed to have been excluded when the Book of Common Prayer divided humanity into the quick and the dead. In time, of course, I learned that "quick" was the ordinary sixteenth-century term for "living," and I learned one thing more: to be wary of a term that appears obvious in its meaning but remains puzzling in its application.

The Shakespeareans' view of Greene has drifted down into the realm of popular culture, and Greene's reputation has suffered the effects. Greene was a native of Norwich, and a few years ago a newspaper there used this kicker in presenting its review of a Shakespeare biography: "The Norwich blaggard who reviled England's greatest poet."

Let's take a closer look at some specifics. "O tiger's heart wrapp'd in a woman's hide!" is the best line in the best speech from a play known in Greene's day as *The True Tragedy of Richard Duke of York.* (The title was changed to *Henry VI, Part Three* when the play was taken into the First Folio of 1623. The recent Oxford University Press edition, however, has restored the original title.) In the play York is tormented by Queen Margaret with the failure of his ambition for the throne and with evidence of the murder of his youngest son, and he responds with an impassioned harangue that constitutes a theatrical *tour de force.* York is put to death by the end of the first act, and for a playgoer that becomes a different sort of true tragedy, since it involves the loss of the play's most vibrant character.

The current scholarly consensus places the origin of *The True Tragedy of Richard Duke of York* in the large company headed by Edward Alleyn. In the period between 1588 (marking the death of Richard Tarlton, the great comic actor who was the star of the Queen's men) and 1594 (the year that the Lord Chamberlain's men was formed, with Richard Burbage as leading actor and William Shakespeare as in-house playwright), Alleyn reigned supreme in the London theatre. He starred in the plays of Greene and his colleagues, including Marlowe's *Tamburlaine the Great,* and opened his 1592 season with Greene's *Friar Bacon and Friar Bungay.*

Alleyn also achieved notable success in the commerce of the entertainment business. He bought the work of writers who were far better educated than he—according to one source Alleyn had been "bred a stage-player"—so any boast regarding writing ability would have justifiably earned a sneering response. Not that it would have slowed Alleyn down very much—with appropriate apologies to Robert Browning, a superstar-mogul's braggadocio should exceed his grasp, or what's a Tinseltown for? Alleyn was noted for a heavy-footed acting style, and an incident that occurred during the 1590-91 season, when a playhouse in which he was performing "cracked," provided a ready target for satire. In addition, there exists documented cause for the ill feeling between Greene and Alleyn.

I intend to show that it was Alleyn who was attacked by Greene as the upstart crow. Since the facts of Alleyn's career are familiar subjects to theatrical scholars, it's a fair question to ask why this solution to the perplexities of *Groat's-worth* has not become a factor in Shakespeare studies. The answer is wrapped up in the hazards of assuming that something is simply obvious—when you're quite sure you *know*, your mind is effectively closed.

Tyrwhitt's discovery of *Groat's-worth* did not, as he had hoped, settle the authorship issue on the *Henry VI* plays; opinions continued to be generated on the subject in great number. Tyrwhitt did have a more lasting effect in highlighting what appeared to him to be the toxin of envy directed at Shakespeare's achievements. Henceforth any perceived irrationalities in *Groat's-worth* could be charged to Greene's account. After all, if Greene's comments were colored by the soul-twisting emotion of envy, who would expect him to be seeing with a clear eye?

Consider, for example, the significance of the "tiger's heart" allusion: this player possesses the heart of a tiger. Could that be Shakespeare? The Shakespeareans explain that, yes, it's Shakespeare, but of course he wasn't at all like that. A nineteenth-century literary historian wrote of "this attack on our untiger-like Shakespeare," and C. L. Barber and Richard P. Wheeler, authors of a book published in 1986, have noted that "Shakespeare's actual role in the theater—to be constantly giving, working within a team, creating parts to realize and nurture the talents of his fellows—is directly counter to Greene's jibe."

It would hardly be a sensible position to sneer at Shakespeare's writing abilities, but that is of little consequence when Greene isn't expected to be making sense. Muriel Bradbrook, a highly distinguished member of the scholarly community, viewed Greene's portrayal of the upstart crow in terms of "the ignorant monster, a sort of Caliban (the monster to end all monsters) tamed and taught language that he turns against his master....Shakespeare for Greene is a species of Caliban." *Shakespeare* as Caliban?

John Dover Wilson and Peter Alexander were eminent twentieth-century scholars who spent decades disputing with each other about *Groat's-worth*, but you can probably guess on which point they were able to agree.

Dover Wilson chose to revive an older theory that viewed *Groat's-worth* as harboring a charge of plagiarism. Yet even as he did so, he readily admitted that any tinkering Shakespeare might have done to the plays of Greene and his colleagues—and the emphasis is on *might*, since no firm evidence exists to show that Shakespeare was doing this in 1592—would have constituted nothing more than "a perfectly normal procedure of the playhouse." To view such actions as plagiarism would mean that Greene "was only making himself ridiculous in the eyes of all who knew the facts." Dover Wilson obviously included himself in that group.

For his part Alexander commented that "in the whole indictment there is no word of plagiarism....The only two accusations made against Shakespeare are that he was an actor, 'an upstart Crow,' and that being this he yet ventured to write plays." What, then, did Shakespeare do to deserve Greene's anger? Alexander thought that Greene would have been concerned with the increased competition Shakespeare could have provided, yet as we will see, Greene was having no trouble finding buyers for his plays; and even when Shakespeare was at the height of his powers the Lord Chamberlain's men performed the work of other writers. "There is little logic in Greene's case," Alexander was forced to conclude, "but he was a disappointed and bitter man."

Gareth Lloyd Evans, author of *The Upstart Crow: An Introduction to Shakespeare's Plays,* explained to his readers that "Greene was an unpredictable, neurotic man, with many chips on his shoulder"; and just as the Ptolemaic astronomers endeavored to keep their geocentric view of the universe functioning by adding invisible spheres as required, the Shakespeareans have always been able to find an additional chip to lay on Greene's ample shoulders.

The "tiger's heart" allusion serves for them as a further example of Greene's irrationality. If the upstart crow is so utterly hopeless as a writer, why would Greene link him to a line that plays so splendidly in the theatre? To be sure, much of the confusion would be gone if the scholars applied to this situation a basic reality of the theatre—that the person who speaks a line on stage is not the person who wrote it. Yet considering that there is no evidence placing Shakespeare in an acting company in 1592, the Shakespearean interpretation would be gone as well.

And so they wallow. John Semple Smart, an influential scholar from the University of Glasgow, chose to concentrate on "the vital significance of the words *with his*" and cited as an example, "When I say, 'Mr. Asquith, with his "Wait and See,"' I mean that it was Mr. Asquith who said 'Wait and See.' I do not mean that I said it, or that it was said by one of my friends, or by anybody but Mr. Asquith."

In the spring of 1910 Prime Minister Herbert Henry Asquith became known for the remark "wait and see!"; the issue was the reintroduction of the budget following its rejection by the House of Lords. Eric Partridge has pointed out that the term was "probably used twenty or thirty years earlier." Asquith, then, did not create it, but there's no question that he made "wait and see!" famous by speaking it in a highly public way.

For Smart, however, Greene's use of *his* in *Groat's-worth* was sufficient indication that the "tiger's heart" line—and hence the entire play—was being attributed to Shakespeare. The sneering at the upstart crow's writing ability would then mean that Greene regarded the line as "pretentious rubbish." Since it is hardly that, this commentary wouldn't seem to make sense, but Smart, writing in the tone of a schoolmaster lecturing a roomful of recalcitrant students, ruled that Greene's "criticism does not matter; what we are concerned with is his evidence." Yet how can anyone come to terms with Greene's evidence without assessing the import of his sneer? Smart's answer was to dabble in wishful thinking: "This passage from Greene has had such a devastating effect on Shakespearian study that we cannot but wish it had never been written or never discovered."

Since it's hardly in a researcher's nature to long for *less* information, you might suppose that this comment would be written off as the result of a momentary pique and otherwise ignored. Not so: Samuel Schoenbaum, one of the leading Shakespeare biographers of our day, included it in his *William Shakespeare: A Documentary Life* with the remark that "one can sympathize with the exasperation voiced by one distinguished commentator in this century."

(It can be noted here that the earliest piece of evidence documenting Shakespeare's membership in an acting company comes with the performances at court by the Lord Chamberlain's men in December, 1594. In addition, Shakespeare was not the company's star.)

The question that needs to be asked is this: what happens when a great actor takes hold of a great line? A process occurs that is rooted in an alchemy of acting and the prerogatives of stardom, and it's a force that even writers recognize: at the 1986 Academy Awards presentation an Oscar winner for Best Original Screenplay thanked the studio for bringing the writers' vision to the screen and added, "As for the vision of the Academy, all I can do is repeat the words of Humphrey Bogart, 'Here's looking at you, kid.' "

*Whose* words? Four people have claimed a share of the screenplay of *Casablanca*—Julius and Philip Epstein, Howard Koch, and Casey Robinson—yet who would argue that in some important sense those are Bogart's words? When a great actor delivers a great line he makes it *his*.

"In comes *Chettle* sweating and blowing, by reason of his fatnes"—that's how a contemporary described an entrance by Henry Chettle. Chettle was a man of letters before he became a minor literary figure of the period—he had worked as a typesetter and a printer—and he enters the *Groat's-worth* controversy as the person responsible for seeing the book into print. When *Groat's-worth* was licensed on September 20, 1592, the publisher took care to include the notation it was being brought out "vppon the perill of Henrye Chettle."

Chettle's version of the trouble that came his way has been preserved in the preface to his *Kind-Heart's Dream*, a book licensed on December 6. There Chettle noted that Greene's "letter written to divers [several] play-makers, is offensiuely by one or two of them taken, and because on the dead they cannot be auenged, they wilfully forge in their conceites a liuing Author: and after tossing it two [to] and fro, no remedy, but it must light on me."

In dealing with the complaints of Christopher Marlowe, one of Greene's fellow playwrights, Chettle was willing to strike a pose of defiance, but when it came to the upstart crow he gave way to gushing: "My self haue seene his demeanor no lesse ciuill than he exelent in the qualitie [profession of acting] he professes: Besides, diuers of worship [several gentlemen] have reported, his vprightnes of dealing, which argues [proves] his honesty, and his facetious [urbane, witty] grace in writting, that approues [confirms] his Art."

So the upstart crow, having first sought to be *avenged* on Chettle, now emerges with civil demeanor, excellent acting skills, honesty, and a new sort of writing ability: instead of being able to bombast out a blank verse, he has become a comic writer. In this sort of save-your-skin exercise one out of four on the truthfulness scale is not so bad.

Since superstar-moguls aren't readers, Chettle was able to set the record straight by burying within the text of *Kind-Heart's Dream* a description of Greene that echoed the very passage that created so much trouble:

> ...Robert Greene, maister of Artes: of whome (howe euer some suppose themselues iniured [injured]) I haue learned to speake, considering he is dead, *nill nisi necessarium* [nothing except what is necessary].
>
> He was of singuler pleasaunce [pleasantry] the verye supporter, and to no mans disgrace bee this intended, the only Comedian of a vulgar [popular] writer in this country.

This establishes that it is Greene who is the real writer—no offense intended to anyone else, of course—and the upstart crow's claim is nothing more than puffery.

Chettle's apology did accomplish its purpose of obscuring harsh realities in a warm, hazy glow. Sir Richard Baker was in his twenties when the *Groat's-worth* controversy broke, and he later praised Alleyn as being "Famous as well for his *Honesty*, as for his *Acting*." A modern scholar named John Briley has looked at Alleyn's handling of his father-in-law's estate and arrived at a rather different view, concluding that Alleyn was "a very shrewd, and often unscrupulous, man with the law"; but, thanks to Chettle's efforts, the private reality was not reflected in the public image.

The Shakespeare biographers, of course, view the apology in an altogether different light; for them Chettle is illuminating their man in glorious rays. "This is the most handsome apology that I know in the Elizabethan age," A. L. Rowse has enthused, while Peter Quennell speculated that Chettle "may have been instantly disarmed by Shakespeare's good-humour and his open, winning manners." The apology also serves as an indicator of the extent of Greene's irrationality. T. W. Baldwin ruled that "the apology to both actor and dramatist is categoric and complete. Greene was wrong on all counts."

Only rarely do Shakespeareans experience any doubts as they bask in the seeming glories of Chettle's splendid words. M. M. Reese thought there was "something disingenuous about the whole passage," yet did not challenge the standard view with his conclusion: "Be that as it may, his apology contains the first contemporary reference to Shakespeare as a man, and it is handsome enough." Of course the handsomeness of the apology is hardly the issue; the degree to which it can claim some sort of correlation to reality very much is.

No conspiracy has ever existed to place Greene's attack within the realm of Shakespeare biography. In spite of all the problems it creates for the Shakespeareans, it has remained there, I believe, because it has proved so useful in dealing with the "lost years," that span between the christening of Shakespeare's twins in Stratford in 1583 and the publication of *Venus and Adonis* in London a decade later. This gap is the black hole of Shakespeare studies, capable of consuming the brightest bursts of speculation. As Russell Fraser, author of *Young Shakespeare,* has observed, "Biographers are grateful to Greene for certifying Shakespeare's presence in London" in 1592.

We can all agree that Greene was attacking a prominent figure in the London theatre; but from there the logic of the Shakespearean position proceeds along this course: Greene was obviously attacking Shakespeare; therefore Shakespeare was a prominent figure at the time of the attack. Yet even in the midst of so much scholarly certainty *Groat's-worth* remains full of enigmas for the Shakespeareans. John Dover Wilson went so far as to comment on Greene's attack and Chettle's apology: "These two references have been quoted and discussed hundreds of times....Nevertheless it is doubtful whether their full meaning has even yet been grasped." The path not taken is to concentrate on Greene's dealings with Alleyn—unquestionably the most powerful figure in the theatre of 1592—and to come to closure on the realities of a writer's discontents in the entertainment business. That means restoring the upstart crow to his rightful measure of mogul-style crudeness and presumption—tiger's heart indeed.

# 2

I OWN AN ATTENUATED, BEATEN, SNIPPED PIECE OF METAL bearing a partially worn image of a steely-eyed Elizabeth I—an old groat, the four-pence coin of the day.

How much "wit" does four pence buy? While it's possible to write an entire essay on the variety of the word's meanings—and C. S. Lewis has done so—for our purposes "wit" can be considered as the type of sense constituent in common sense. Indeed, at one time "common wit" was a synonym of "common sense," although today the word finds a survival chiefly in compounds—add a moiety of wit and a "half-wit" becomes wise.

Greene's Letter to the Playwrights comes toward the end of *Groat's-worth*; the first part of the book is an example of the quasi-autobiographical narrative he often wrote. The protagonist here is one Roberto, who receives as his sole bequest from his wealthy father "an old groat, (being y^e^ [the] stocke I first began with) wherewith I wish him to buy a groats-worth of wit." The father's anger is not unwarranted; at a dinner party Roberto had taken the opportunity to inveigh against usury, "knowing his father and most of the company to be execrable vsurers."

Roberto's brother receives an inheritance that makes him wealthy, and Roberto's attempt to defraud him results in his receiving Jack Drum's entertainment—thc Elizabethan equivalent of the bum's rush. Being a poet, he versifies his complaints, and a stranger approaches with an offer of help. "Men of my profession," the newcomer assures Roberto, "gette by schollers their whole liuing."

Roberto is astonished to discover that he is talking to an actor: "I tooke you rather for a Gentleman of great liuing" (i.e., one with a large estate). The player responds that he is "reputed able at my proper [own] cost to build a Windmill." Whatever that may mean, a windmill would be an appropriate structure for someone who is as much a blowhard as the player. There was a day when he carried his pack "a footebacke"—the jest here is that you go on footback (i.e., walk) when you can't afford to ride on horseback—but *"Tempora mutantur* [the times are changing], I know you know the meaning of it better than I, but I thus conster [construe] it, its otherwise now; for my very share in playing apparell will not be sold for two hundred pounds."

"Truly (said *Roberto*) tis straunge, that you should so prosper in that vayne practise, for that it seemes to mee your voice is nothing gratious."

"Nay then, saide the Player, I mislike your iudgement: why, I am as famous for Delphrigus, & the King of Fairies, as euer was any of my time." These titles are indicative of the plays of an earlier day. "The twelue labors of Hercules haue I terribly thundred on the Stage, and plaid three Scenes of the Deuill in the High way to heauen." In addition, for a seven-year span, the ordinary period of an apprenticeship, he "was absolute Interpreter to the puppets"—one who provided voices for a puppet show.

And the player can do more: "I can serue to make a pretie speech, for I was a countrey Author, passing at a

Morrall [a morality play], for twas I that pende the Morrall of mans witte, the Dialogue of Diues." This represents another type of outmoded material: the morality plays, which featured Biblical themes, were mainstays of the medieval theatre. Surely it is no accident that this player's work features Dives, the rich man in the story of Lazarus.

"But now my Almanacke is out of date:

> *The people make no estimation,*
> *Of Morrals teaching education.*

Was not this prettie for a plaine rime extempore? if ye will ye shall haue more."

"Nay its enough, said *Roberto*, but how mean you to vse mee?"

"Why sir, in making Playes," the player responds, "for which you shall be well paid, if you will take the paines."

Note that the actor who so boasts of his playwriting skills recruits a well-educated person to write for him. Taking up residence in the metropolis, Roberto soon finds himself famous as "an Arch-plaimaking-poet," even though he acquires the habit of taking advances and not delivering the finished work. "It becoms me," he boasts, "to bee contrary to the worlde; for commonly when vulgar men receiue earnest [money], they doo performe, when I am paid any thing afore-hand, I breake my promise." And in case the reader should miss the point, Greene states that Roberto's life was "in most parts agreeing with" his own.

Well, no one ever said that tinsel builds character. Instead of occupying a place in a nobleman's retinue, with his creations duly admired by a leading member of society, Greene was writing for people who gauged his achievement by the number of paying customers it brought in.

Another 1592 publication reveals how he responded to

the situation. After the Queen's men purchased *Orlando Furioso* from him and went on tour, Greene sold the play a second time to Alleyn's company. This was his reported justification for the fraud:

> There was no more faith to be held with Plaiers, then with them that valued faith at the price of a feather: for as they were *Comœdians* to act, so the actions of their liues were *Cameleon* like, that they were vncertaine, variable, time pleasers, men that measured honestie by profite, and that regarded their Authors not by desart [worth], but by necessitie of time.

Whatever can be said for Greene's sense of morality, it may be noted that the realities of working in the entertainment business haven't changed very much. During a 1978 meeting at United Artists to discuss major acquisitions Christopher Mankiewicz, the son of a renowned director and nephew of the screenwriter of *Citizen Kane*, gave vent to his feelings about an item under consideration: "Fellas, this book is a piece of *shit!*" Danny Rissner, UA's head of production, agreed but added, "It's not about whether it's a piece of shit or it's not a piece of shit. It's about whether we want to make a goddamn deal."

"On this unmitigated, irredeemable piece of *shit?*"

Ignoring Mankiewicz's outburst, Rissner borrowed matches and proceeded to light a cigarette. He then asked the meeting, "What's the minimum bid we could make, you think? A million? A million five?"

Cheat Alleyn and you get Alleyn Furioso. Out of Tamburlaine's maw words flowed forth; speaking from his outraged pride Alleyn said the one thing that was guaranteed to get under the skin of a refractory writer: *I can bombast out a blank verse as well as the best of you.* The hot type of

*Groat's-worth* reveals that however wide of the mark Alleyn's statement was, it was eminently successful in getting Greene angry as hell.

# 3

A SUPPOSED PORTRAIT OF CHRISTOPHER MARLOWE AT AGE 21 bears the motto "Quod Me Nutrit Me Destruit"—*that which nourishes me is destroying me*—a cry from the heart by a young man seized with a splendid poetic sensibility. In Greene's case, however, the forces of destruction took the more mundane forms of wine and womanizing.

Greene received B.A. and M.A. degrees at Cambridge, and an additional M.A. from Oxford enabled him to announce on the title pages of his books that he was *Utriusque Academiae in Artibus Magister*—Master of Arts in Both Universities. His writings are largely free of the profusion of sexual innuendo and bawdy punning that Shakespeare favored; here love exists somewhere between a pure passion and a morbid condition. It was otherwise in his life: Greene left his wife and child to come to London, and he took up residence with a prostitute whose brother was the well-known criminal Cutting Ball. She gave birth to a son who was christened with the starkly-inappropriate name of Fortunatus Greene; the child died in infancy. Even though Greene racked up debts everywhere, he managed to own a sleeved cloak of goose-turd green, a hue much favored by fancy dressers, while an occasionally-nurtured religious sensibility served chiefly to remind him that he was unable to live within the bounds prescribed by preachers.

In the summer of 1592 Greene became ill after consuming a "surfeit" of pickled herring and Rhenish wine. Penniless, he took refuge in the home of a Dowgate shoemaker and during this period experienced one final conversion. Fortunatus' mother and another woman came to visit, but the actors who had so sweet-talked him earlier were nowhere to be found. He died on September 3. The shoemaker's wife laid a garland of bays on his head, the honor accorded poets in classical times, and burial followed in a pauper's grave.

While any writer might hope that his work would survive him, there is a particular immediacy in the Letter to the Playwrights. In wishing for his colleagues that "spend their wits in making plaies...a better exercise, and wisdome to preuent his extremities," Greene expressed the hope that they could profit from his experience. The religious element is particularly prominent in the comments directed to the first playwright, who is addressed as "thou famous gracer of Tragedians" and is universally accepted as Marlowe. Greene criticized Marlowe's flirtation with atheism and might-makes-right philosophies, and there was something else in the text as well, which Chettle chose to delete. Many commentators have thought that this was a reference to Marlowe's homosexuality.

The second playwright, addressed as "yong *Iuuenall*" (young Juvenal), and assumed, with not quite the same level of agreement, to be Nashe, received a warning against using his satirical gifts to deliver personal attacks. It was a plea that went for naught: Nashe was the holder of a black belt in the Martial arts and showed himself to be an unrepentant Juvenal offender in the events that followed Greene's death. Greene mentioned a comedy that the second playwright "lastly with mee together writ," but as none of Nashe's work for the adult theatre has survived, this reference is impossible to trace.

Greene's third colleague has been "driuen (as my selfe) to extreme shifts." What is important for the identification here is the statement, "Were it not an idolatrous oth, I would sweare by sweet S[t]. George...." In the second edition of *Groat's-worth* the typesetter placed the proper name in the equivalent of italics, and scholars have agreed that Greene was writing to George Peele, a prolific playwright who was noted for living in dire poverty. In Greene's eyes Peele was undeserving of better luck since he depended "on so meane a stay [source of support]."

"Base minded men all three of you," Greene wrote, "if by my miserie you be not warnd"—particularly so because the actors had not sought out these writers as they had Greene. To heap insult on his adversaries Greene placed them with two of the lowest categories of performers: "Those Puppets...that spake from our mouths, those Anticks garnisht in our colours." Antics were grotesque figures with animal heads used for blustering satire.

"Is it not strange, that I, to whom they all haue beene beholding," Greene asked, "is it not like that you, to whome they all haue beene beholding, shall (were yee in that case as I am now) bee both at once of them forsaken?" "Both" takes in Greene on the one hand, writing from his sickbed with no aid forthcoming from the actors, and the three playwrights on the other, who may expect to be treated in similar fashion.

How does a tycoon deal with a talented and rebellious underling? The archetypal response of the Hollywood mogul was to shout, "Keep that bastard off the lot—until I tell you I need him." John Dover Wilson stressed the idea that a boycott was instituted against Greene as a result of the double sale of *Orlando Furioso*. It's a likely possibility, but the challenge for an upholder of Shakespearean orthodoxy on *Groat's-worth* was to find some sort of role for Shakespeare in this controversy between Greene and Alleyn. "We do not know either whether Shakespeare had anything to do with discovering the practice or with the boycott which almost certainly followed," Dover Wilson admitted; but if Shakespeare were somehow involved, Greene might have found it satisfying to have something to throw back at him. That, Dover Wilson believed, was the unreasonable charge of plagiarism.

Yet because this scenario, as inventive as it is, cannot account for the depth of Greene's anger, Dover Wilson wondered if there were some other issue, perhaps "a failure to respond to a last appeal for help"—something, at least, that could account for a situation in which Greene in an attack on actors "seems to point at Shakespeare as the most callous of them all."

In fact, the source of the problem is an old dispute and a modern one as well. The playwright in *All About Eve* spoke for all those who write for stars when he shouted at Margo Channing, "I shall never understand the weird process by which a body with a voice suddenly fancies itself as a mind!...It's about time the piano realized it has not written the concerto!"

Greene's message to his colleagues is the same sort of advice that F. Scott Fitzgerald dispensed to screenwriter Nunnally Johnson: "Listen, Nunnally, get out of Hollywood. It will ruin you. You have a talent—you'll kill it here." In Greene's words: "O that I might intreat your rare wits to be imploied in more profitable courses: & let those

Apes imitate [perform] your past excellence, and neuer more acquaint them with your admired inuentions [creations]."

Greene added that he was certain that the thriftiest of his colleagues would never prove to be a usurer, "and the kindest of them all will neuer proue a kind nurse: yet whilest you may, seeke you better Maisters; for it is pittie men of such rare wits, should be subiect to the pleasure of such rude groomes." In other words, find a patron and go write the great English poem, just as you've always talked of doing. And don't let them tell you how much they love ya, baby: "When they sooth you with tearms of Maistership, remember *Robert Greene*, whome they haue often so flattered, perishes now for want of comfort [support]."

# 4

NOW LET'S TAKE A LOOK AT WHAT WENT INTO GREENE'S attack and how it has been interpreted.

## "...upstart..."

"Upstart" was still a relatively new word when Greene used it. A text dating from 1555 offered the observation, "These gentlemen are nowe called vpstartes, a terme lately inuented by such as pondered not y^e [the] grounds of honest meanes of rising or commyng to promocion." Greene employed the term extensively in another 1592 book, *A Quip for an Upstart Courtier*, where he inveighed against "proud and vnmannerly vpstarts" and described one of the book's central characters as "an vpstart come out of *Italy*, begot of Pride, nursed vp by selfe love, & brought into this country by his companion Nufanglenesse [newfangledness]."

The linking of "upstart" to pride can be seen in other examples from the period. Holinshed's *Chronicles* noted that during Edward II's reign Hugh Spencer was opposed by the nobles because he bore himself "so hautie and proude"; in Marlowe's *Edward II* Spencer is included in the category of "pernitious upstarts." Elsewhere in the play Warwick asks, "Think you that we can brooke this upstart pride?" In *1 Henry VI* Joan of Arc describes Sir William

Lucy as an "upstart" who "speaks with such a proud commanding spirit"; an editor has glossed "upstart" as "overbearing fellow."

## "...an upstart crow..."

Alleyn was born in 1566 in the London parish of St. Botolph's, Bishopsgate. His father was an innkeeper who died when Alleyn was a child; his mother then married a haberdasher. Her maiden name was Townley, and Alleyn once claimed, without much evidence, that she was related to the distinguished Townley family of Lancashire. But Alleyn achieved a pedigree of his own within the acting profession: at age nineteen he was listed third on the warrant provided by the Earl of Worcester for his players and he later headed the Admiral's men.

Alleyn's company moved to Philip Henslowe's Rose playhouse for its 1592 season, and in October of that year the star married Henslowe's stepdaughter, Joan Woodward. The letters that Alleyn later wrote to "my good sweett mouse" show that there was considerable affection in the marriage, but it's also clear that the match ensured his prosperity. No longer would he just be the leading actor-manager of the day; now he would be Henslowe's partner as well. Eventually he was in a position to engage in a major act of philanthropy, the founding of the College of God's Gift. In addition to educating needy students, the institution provided housing for the poor, making it in the parlance of the day a "hospital." The school is still in existence; today it is known as Dulwich College.

Joan Alleyn died in June, 1623, and was buried in the school's chapel. Before the year was out Alleyn had married Constance Donne, the twenty-year-old daughter of John Donne, the dean of St. Paul's Cathedral. The bride's father pushed for the marriage to be performed without delay; he had been stricken with a life-threatening fever and, as any parent of the time might, wanted to be certain that his daughter had found a husband. It was during a protracted convalescence that Donne composed the memorable meditation, "No man is an island..."

Once his recovery was complete, however, Donne encountered some difficulties with his new son-in-law. (Alleyn was actually the elder of the two men.) We have only one side of the story, the draft of a letter in which Alleyn presented a litany of complaints; presumably a final copy was written and sent, although neither it nor a reply is extant.

The trouble had flared up when Donne refused to provide a promised loan of £500. While that was a substantial sum of money, for Alleyn it represented that "comon curtesie afforded to a frend, I mean y[e] [the] Loane off [of] vnvseful moneys." After being denied the sum, Alleyn recalled that he told Donne that "I now perceued you esteemd £500 beefor my honesty[,] your own reputacon [reputation] or your daughter['s] good." At the time an angry Donne responded twice that the accusation was false and a lie.

Donne had once called Alleyn a plain man. In his letter Alleyn remembered that remark and proceeded to use humility as a bludgeon: "I desire allways so to be for I thank god I never Could disguise in my Lyfe & I am to owld now to lerne...my hart & tong must goe to gather....Therfore sinc I am willing to be so & your knowled[ge] longe howldeth itt I pray you pardon such faultes as my Illetterat pleyness [plainness] Comittes." Donne's biographer has commented that "both he and Alleyn were obviously quick-tempered men."

In a sermon for Candlemas Day, February 2 of a year unspecified, Dean Donne spoke on the doing of good works, and it may be that he had someone rather specific in mind:

> They are not your works, if that you give be not your owne. Nor is it your own, if it were ill gotten at first....First let that that was ill gotten, be deducted, and restored, and then, of the rest, which is truly thine owne, give cheerefully....Till this defalcation [deduction], this scrutiny be made, that you know what's your owne, what's other mens, as your Tombe shall be but a monument of your rotten bones, how much gold or marble soever be bestowed upon it, so that Hospitall, that free-schoole, that Colledge that you shall build, and endow, will bee but a monument of your bribery, your extortion, your oppression; and God, who will not be in debt, (though he owe you nothing that built it) may be pleased to give the reward of all that, to them, from whom that which was spent upon it, was unjustly taken.

## "...the glory of others' feathers..."

In *Francesco's Fortunes* (1590) Greene offered a commentary on the theatre of the classical world as a way of illuminating the contemporary setting. Acting, he noted, was originally the preserve of "men of great honor and graue account"; then the professionals took over and "grewe not onely excellent, but rich and insolent." The celebrated Roman actor Roscius even went so far as to compare his skills to Cicero's,

> which insolencie made the learned Orator to growe into these termes; why *Roscius*, art thou proud with *Esops*

> Crow, being pranct [decked out] with the glorie of others feathers? of thy selfe thou canst say nothing, and if the Cobler hath taught thee to say *Aue Cæsar,* disdain not thy tutor, because thou pratest in a Kings chamber: what sentence thou vtterest on the stage, flowes from the censure [judgment] of our wittes, and what sentence or conceipte of the inuention [creation] the people applaud for excellent, that comes from the secrets of our knowledge. I graunt your action, though it be a kind of mechanical labour; yet wel done tis worthie of praise: but you worthlesse, if for so small a toy you waxe proud. At this *Roscius* waxt red, and bewraied [exposed] his imperfection with silence.

Roscius has mastered "action"—the language of gesture that was an integral part of performance—but in this piece of writer's wish fulfillment he has been put in his place by one who has mastered words.

The account of the rivalry between Cicero and Roscius is in Macrobius' *Saturnalia*, although Greene invented the reply by Cicero. Macrobius is also the source for the story of the crow trained by a cobbler to offer greetings to Augustus Caesar. Greene found it useful to combine that bird with Aesop's crow to establish the point that a star is nothing more than a crow dependent upon the plumage created by his writers. Perceptive readers of the day may also have made the connection that Marlowe, Alleyn's leading writer, was the son of a cobbler—and that, of course, gets into the issue of the identity of Roscius.

"Roscius here stands for Alleyn," Schoenbaum has stated in *William Shakespeare: A Documentary Life*; and Peter Alexander noted that "Greene uses the same terms in describing Alleyn as he does in his attack on Shakespeare." There is, as Alexander pointed out, a difference: the upstart crow of *Groat's-worth* supposes he can bombast out a blank verse. For a Shakespearean commentator, of course, that new twist could never function as the latest horror story from the star with the largest ego. No—Greene's comment, stripped of its sneering force, is reduced to serving as a helpful piece of information for identifying Shakespeare as the upstart crow. In all of this the point that goes unconsidered is: *same terms, same target.*

### "...for there is an upstart crow, beautified with our feathers..."

Elizabethans spoke of going to *hear* a play rather than see a play, so for a moment imagine the great star in his glorious raiment—not costumes, but splendid plumes of pentameter highlighted by brightly-hued bursts of similes and the patterned weaving of alliteration. Then view in his wake the poor artificer who has cut and stitched, snipped and crafted the sheer weight of verbalisms underpinning the luminary's glory. All the star has to do is *say* the words...

"It is admitted," a friendly biographer of Alleyn wrote in the late nineteenth century, "that he was not a man of very high culture; but, as an actor at the head of his profession, his pronunciation must have been accurate according to the standard of the day."

Let's look at some feathers. Alleyn had the leading roles in Marlowe's best plays, dominating the stage as Tamburlaine, Faustus, and Barabas in *The Jew of Malta.* As I've noted, he opened his 1592 season at the Rose with Greene's *Friar Bacon and Friar Bungay*; it was a popular play that managed to combine a tale of necromancy with a prince-meets-girl romance. Included in Alleyn's papers at Dulwich

College is the role of Orlando in *Orlando Furioso.* While most of the text is written in the slow-paced hand of a scrivener, some corrections and an occasional entire line are in Alleyn's fluid, forward-slanting handwriting.

In Peele's *Battle of Alcazar* Alleyn played the starring role of the Moorish warlord Muly Mahamet; and Peele is also linked to Alleyn in a piece of Elizabethan fan mail. It's a letter written by one W. P. urging Alleyn to accept the proffered terms of an acting competition with two older actors, Bentley and Knell. A handicap seems to have been imposed upon Alleyn: while he would be free to select "any one playe, that either Bentley or Knell plaide," he could not use material from his writer, Peele. W. P. was ready to bet on Alleyn and promised to share not only half his winnings but to add a crown (five shillings) as well:

> Deny me not sweete Nedd, the wager's downe,
> and twice as muche, commaunde of me or myne:
> And if you wynne J sweare the half is thyne;
> and for an ouerplus, an English Crowne.
> Appoint the tyme, and stint [apportion] it as you pleas,
> Your labor's gaine; and that will proue it ease.

Elizabethan actors were always ready to strut their stuff—Hamlet said to one of the players visiting Elsinore, "Come, give us a taste of your quality. Come, a passionate speech"—but the outcome of this competition remains unknown.

As might be expected, when the Shakespeareans look at the upstart crow, they see a bird of a different feather. I've mentioned the debate within their ranks as to whether Greene was complaining of plagiarism. One of Horace's *Epistles* employs the image of a bird with borrowed plumes in making an accusation of literary theft. John Dover Wilson produced a citing thereof, but two other leading scholars saw no such accusation lurking within Greene's realm. E. K. Chambers ruled that "beautified with our feathers" was "a mere variation" of "garnisht in our colours" in the reference to antics, while Peter Alexander commented that "the phrase used of Shakespeare only points to him as that opprobrious thing to Greene, an actor." For his part Alexander found *Groat's-worth* to be "a pathetic document," adding, "It is unnecessary to criticize its incoherence, or the strange connection between the wages of sin and the payments of the actors."

Clearly Alexander was not well-versed in the literature of Tinseltown. In a thousand forms the writer prostituting his talent has become an entertainment business cliché, and Greene's gripings should be placed alongside the accounts of Fitzgerald, Faulkner, and all those lesser talents out there in La-La Land.

# 5

## "The tiger then hideth his crabbed countenance..."

The expression "crocodile tears" has entered the language to denote a false show of sympathy for a victim, but a similar piece of proverbial wisdom regarding the duplicity of tigers has largely been lost. George Pettie, an Elizabethan writer, noted that "the tiger...haleth the lambe to bee devoured." That's the "hail" of "hail-fellow well-met," an expression that originated in the period.

Greene expressed the notion this way: "The Tyger then hideth his crabbed countenance, when he meaneth to take his pray [prey]: and a man doth most dissemble when he speakes fayrest." He also asked in rhetorical fashion, "When the Tygre hunteth for his pray, doth he then hide his clawes?" After Greene's death the writer of a play entitled *Wily Beguiled* added an echoing of *Groat's-worth* to this theme:

> Well, trust him not: the Tiger hides his clawes
> When oft he doth pretend [plan] the greatest guiles.

It was not by accident that Greene chose "tiger's heart" from *Richard Duke of York.* An actor named Emrys James played York in the Royal Shakespeare Company's 1977-78 production of *Henry VI* and had this to say of the character:

"He is a great wheeler-dealer, yet success fills him with fear.... He is cruel, selfish, a man with an unusually narrow view. He has a naive, simple, and constant desire for power, always seeking, as he says, 'occasions to rise.' "

"...with his *Tygers hart wrapt in a Players hyde.*"

Here is Briley describing Alleyn in action as his father-in-law was dying: "The scene...was evidently one colored thickly in the ugly hues of greed, subterfuge, and hate. In this clouded scene, the great actor...walked only as Mr. Edward Alleyn, but he needed no playwright to fill it with drama and the disturbing presence of human weakness and evil."

James on playing York: "After the death scene I am almost always ill. I actually vomit. Once I was ill just before it. I have been afraid that I will be ill right on stage, for the feeling of nausea is very strong. *Nothing* like this has ever happened to me before."

## ***"...player's hide..."***

"Greene was not writing for scholars," Muriel Bradbrook has cogently remarked; "the context evoked a direct visual memory for his readers." While this comment was made as part of a discussion of antics, it works far better when directed at the theatricality of the "tiger's heart" line.

A few years back I attended a *Henry VI* marathon at a summer Shakespeare festival that was loaded with amateurs—clearly not one of those productions that have been hailed for reviving interest in the plays. After the performance of *Part Two* I overheard one of my fellow playgoers say, "Some of that stuff is so soporific, especially on top of wine. Wine and *Henry VI* is a guaranteed sleep-maker." On the next day, however, an actor who was too young for the part of York—with clumsily-grayed hair and attired in armor that looked like it came from Kmart—seized the stage as he spat out "O tiger's heart wrapp'd in a woman's hide!" Then none of the concerns about acting skills mattered: in the full light of a late summer's day the actor became York, and York held us.

Elizabethan actors were required by law to have a patron, and Alleyn was for many years servant to the Lord High Admiral. In the early 1590s he engineered a merger with Lord Strange's men in which he retained his affiliation as an Admiral's man while the company as a whole generally continued to be known as Strange's men. The publisher of *A Knack to Know a Knave*, a play that premiered in 1592, simplified the complexities of patronage by noting on the title page that it had "bene played by ED. ALLEN and his Companie."

When *Richard Duke of York* was published in 1595, it was attributed theatrically to the Earl of Pembroke's men; presumably that was the last company to have performed it. The text, however, shows clear signs of being an unauthorized publication. Much, though not all, of the verse exists in a mangled state, a situation that puzzled scholars until Peter Alexander set forth a convincing explanation in 1929 in which he argued that some of the actors from the play remembered as much as they could and sold the resulting text to a publisher. Obviously these pirates of Pembroke's did not possess a clean text of the play.

In 1593 Henslowe had responded to a request by Alleyn for information about the company by indicating in a letter that the actors had returned to London during a time of plague. Unable to meet expenses on the road, they were pawning their apparel; but despite those straitened circumstances, the company did not offer the play to a publisher. Presumably, then, it was not theirs to offer; yet as a minor company Pembroke's had been able to perform some major plays, including *Edward II*, *Titus Andronicus*, and *The First Part of the Contention between the Two Famous Houses of York and Lancaster*, the companion piece to *Richard Duke of York* that was taken into the First Folio as *Henry VI, Part Two.* The *Contention* underwent a similar sort of unauthorized publication in 1594.

The leading opinion on Pembroke's men was formulated by E. K. Chambers in 1923. While admitting that he was forced to "enter a region of conjecture," Chambers noted that he found it "likely that the origin of Pembroke's men is to be explained by the special conditions of the plague-years 1592-3, and was due to a division for travelling purposes of the large London company formed by the amalgamation of Strange's and the Admiral's." Having an additional patron would have allowed another grouping of actors to go on tour, an important consideration in perilous times. Chambers commented, "Probably some play-books, formerly in use by the Alleyn company, were handed over as an outfit for the new venture, and included...*3 Henry VI.*"

Discoveries regarding the Elizabethan theatre are discouragingly difficult to come by, but in 1974 Mary Edmond announced that she had found the will of a previously unknown actor who seems to have been a member of Pembroke's men. In assessing the significance of her find Edmond concluded that it "strongly supports" the view presented by Chambers.

One thing more needs to be dealt with. A hazard of Elizabethan theatre research lies in discovering that the piece of documentation you would like to have often is simply not to be found. Details of casting for individual productions are extremely difficult to come by, and of the hundreds, perhaps thousands, of roles that Alleyn played, specific documentary evidence exists for only seven. No cast list or prompter's plot (a guide for getting actors on and off the stage) has survived to place Alleyn in the role of York. So the question must be: when a superstar possesses the power to determine who will have the most important part in a play, what are the odds that he will meekly turn it over to a junior member of his company?

For the Shakespeareans Greene's use of the "tiger's heart" line is a major foundation stone in their interpretation of *Groat's-worth*; but let's examine just how solid it actually is. As I've noted, Tyrwhitt's discovery of *Groat's-worth* did nothing to determine in a final way the authorship of the *Henry VI* plays. For convenience the two sides in the ongoing debate may be termed the revisionists and the creationists. For many years the revisionists held the upper hand, so much so that by the late nineteenth and early twentieth centuries editors of *Henry VI* were routinely apportioning the plays to Elizabethan dramatists on the basis of perceived stylistic similarities.

Alexander included a creationist point of view in his 1929 book, yet the strength of his argument was in following the course of the *Contention* and *Richard Duke of York* from performances by a secondary company to anonymous, unauthorized publication. On the basis of the printed texts available, anyone might be expected to favor the angelic quires of the Folio over the sans-seraph tangle of the bad quartos, yet in making such a choice Alexander felt that he was able to state a case for Shakespearean authorship. The alternative, of course, is to view the published *Contention* and *Richard Duke of York* as imperfect renderings of the plays' earliest—and unpublished—versions. That, however, puts us at a further remove from a discernible link to Shakespeare.

While Alexander was able to give the creationist position fresh life, the revisionists have not been silenced. In its 1963-64 season the Royal Shakespeare Company presented Peter Hall's production of *The Wars of the Roses,* an abridgement and adaptation of *Henry VI* and *Richard III.* Hall had asked John Barton to piece together the text, and Barton later commented that he came to view the *Henry VI* plays of the First Folio as "the adaptation and partial revision of some earlier texts (whose nature and authorship we can only guess at) undertaken by Shakespeare to make them part of a cycle which was completed by his *Richard III.*" He added, "I believe that Shakespeare's revision was fitful, pragmatic and hasty, and that the result is not something of which he would have claimed 'this cycle is more or less as I want it,' but rather 'it will serve.' "

That sort of uncertainty also exists in scholarly circles. In the *Textual Companion* to the Oxford University Press' new Shakespeare edition Gary Taylor has noted that "many scholars have doubted Shakespeare's authorship of the entirety of *Richard Duke of York.*" He concluded that "pending further investigation Shakespeare's responsibility for every scene of the play should be regarded as uncertain."

Consider, then, a representative response to *Groat's-*

*worth* from a leading Shakespearean: Schoenbaum has commented, "The 'tiger's heart' alludes sneeringly to a line in Shakespeare's *3 Henry VI*: 'O tiger's heart wrapp'd in a woman's hide!' About the object of Greene's venom there can be no doubt."

*No doubt?* If we can't be certain that Shakespeare wrote the "tiger's heart" line, then it constitutes begging the question—taking as a premise what has not been proved—to use Greene's reference to identify Shakespeare as the upstart crow. Even within the limitations of the Shakespearean position—which views Greene as making a literary, not a theatrical, allusion—this should have been cause enough for serious doubts; but as long as the upstart crow is viewed as being obviously Shakespeare, any doubts that may arise can be expected to do what they've always done for the Shakespeareans.

They'll simply evanesce.

# 6

## "...supposes he is as well able to bombast out a blank verse as the best of you..."

Viewed within the context of the entertainment business there's nothing particularly surprising about this remark. A veteran Hollywood producer has commented that "most studio executives fancy themselves as screenwriters, or at least as impeccable judges of fine writing." What is surprising is that one of my predecessors in the Alleynian position committed the same error as the Shakespeareans: she failed to take Greene's sneer seriously.

A. D. Wraight, author of *In Search of Christopher Marlowe*, a pictorial biography published in 1965, made use of *Groat's-worth* in an unconvincing attempt at placing Greene and Alleyn among the writers of *1 Henry VI*. On a separate point Wraight stated her belief that serious consideration should be given to the notion that Marlowe did not die in 1593, but instead lived on in seclusion to write Shakespeare's plays. She found it disappointing that "it is evident from the attitude of the united front of Shakespearean scholars that Marlowe would only be of interest to them dead in 1593, not living in 1594." Since I'm opposed to the Shakespeare-didn't-write-Shakespeare's-plays fantasias, this opinion affords me the novel experience of taking my place in the united front.

### "...being an absolute *Johannes factotum...*"

What goes into making an absolute Johnny Do-All of the theatre? Start with the head of London's largest and most important acting company; grant him a skill in an allied field—the earliest document showing an occupation for Alleyn, dating from 1595, lists him as a musician—and then have him marry Philip Henslowe's step-daughter. That would be enough to transform anyone into a Johnny Do-All; but now that Alleyn, by his own admission, can *write,* Greene wants to make it sneeringly clear that he must be something more: an *absolute* Johnny Do-All.

I always find it intriguing when the Shakespeare scholars look past a connection to Alleyn in order to find a place for Shakespeare in *Groat's-worth.* Henslowe was noteworthy among his contemporaries as a moneylender to the underclass of the entertainment world, and E. A. J. Honigmann has offered the comment:

> Greene's "Tyger's hart," together with "greedy miser" and "Vsurer," conjures up a picture that is already familiar to students of Elizabethan drama—that of Philip Henslowe, the theatrical entrepreneur who helped out as banker for various groups of actors from 1592 and also carried on a lucrative business as pawnbroker or, as contemporaries will have said, as usurer.

While this statement effectively places the lair of the tiger within Henslowe's household, it's not much help for a Shakespearean solution to *Groat's-worth*'s puzzlements. So Honigmann proceeded to "tentatively suggest" that Shakespeare might have functioned in a Henslowe-like manner during the 1590-94 period, even though no evidence exists to show that he was doing anything of the sort at the time Greene was writing *Groat's-worth.*

As could be expected, the Shakespeare biographers offer a range of opinions on "absolute *Johannes factotum.*" Ivor Brown paraphrased the term as "Jack-of-all-trades, author as well as actor," while Anthony Burgess commented, "The *Johannes factotum*, Johnny Do-all or Jack-of-all-trades, refers to the play-mending, speech-vamping, walking-on Will who has now bloomed into a dramatic poet whose lines are memorable." Yet a Swiss critic named Hanspeter Born has countered that "Shakespeare for Greene is an *absolute* Johannes fac totum, not a Jack-of-two-trades but a Jack-of-all-trades." While that supplies a somewhat better rendering of Greene's point, Born's formulation turns out to be a pale concoction—in this view Shakespeare had enlarged his franchise by revising a play that Born attributes to Greene.

John Dover Wilson viewed *Johannes factotum* as having much more limited application. He thought that Greene was crediting Shakespeare with being a successful writer whose "plays are of many kinds (for so I interpret 'Johannes factotum')." But A. L. Rowse chose to look at Greene's statement from the vantage point provided by the culmination of Shakespeare's career: "William Shakespeare in the end was a complete man of the theatre: player, dramatist, producer, part-owner, sharer of profits. A perfect Johannes Factotum, as Robert Greene said."

Any theory on *Groat's-worth*, however, should not have to credit Greene with prescience in order to work. All that can be said about Shakespeare in 1592 is that he may have been an actor and he may be have been a playwright—it depends on which set of speculations you want to follow. Shakespeare did become a sharer—what we would term a general partner—in the Lord Chamberlain's men, which was formed in the summer of 1594. He also acquired a ten percent interest in the Globe when it was built in 1599, but he was never the leading actor of his company. In a theatrical environment accustomed to actor-managers, artistic control would have been in the hands of Richard Burbage.

Viewed in a certain light, the Lord Chamberlain's men could be accused of a parochial outlook. True, their in-house playwright created some of the world's outstanding plays, but they showed scant interest in the entire spectrum of Southwark amusements. That was not the case with Alleyn, who through an investment made in 1594 was to come into association with such celebrities as Harry Hunks, George Stone, and Sackerson. The care and feeding of these stars was a little different: they were bears who performed at the Bear Garden, London's leading bear-baiting arena. The structure deteriorated over time, and in 1613 it was replaced by the Hope, a dual-purpose facility with a removable stage that allowed it to be used for both plays and bear-baitings. Southwark was famous for yet another type of entertainment—the stews (houses of prostitution)—and Alleyn had investments there as well. Four of his establishments were included in his will as a bequest to Dulwich College.

In 1600 Alleyn and Henslowe built the Fortune playhouse on a site north of the City near Golden (or Golding) Lane. This was a matter of keeping up with the competition, as a year earlier the Chamberlain's men had moved south and erected the Globe near the decaying Rose. Alleyn and

Henslowe hired the carpenter who had overseen the construction of the Globe and instructed him to match in various points what he had done there. The overall shape was different, however: instead of the Globe's "wooden O," the Fortune was square.

Alleyn had retired from acting three years earlier, but the new playhouse lured him back onto the stage. The Fortune received a ringing endorsement from the Privy Council, which noted that the Queen "hath sondrye tymes signified her pleasuer" that Alleyn should begin acting again; and Alleyn managed to win over local residents by promising "to give a very liberall porcion of money weekelie, towards y^e^ [the] releef of our Poore."

In the new reign the Lord Chamberlain's men took top billing as the King's men while Alleyn's company became Prince Henry's men. For King James' coronation procession through London on March 15, 1604, Alleyn delivered a speech as *Genius Urbi* (the spirit of the city); according to one account, it was performed "with excellent Action, and a well tun'de audible voyce."

Two days earlier the royal family had witnessed an exotic variant of bear-baiting. The king had become intrigued with the lions housed in the Tower of London, and a chronicler noted that he asked Alleyn "to fetch secretly three of the fellest [fiercest] dogs in the Garden." When the first dog was placed in the lions' den, he immediately "flew to the face of the Lion, but the Lyon suddenly shooke him off, & graspt him fast by the neck, drawing the dog vp staires & downe staires." The next dog to enter the fray received similar treatment.

> Whereupon the King commanded the third dog to be put in before the second dog was spoyled, which third dogge

> more fierce and fell then eyther of the former, and in despight either of clawes or strength, tooke the Lyon by the lippe, but the Lyon so tore the dog by the eyes, head, and face, that he lost his hold, and then the Lyon tooke the Dogs necke in his mouth, drawing him vp and downe as hee did the former, but being wearied, could not bite so deadly as at the first....
>
> You shall understand the last two dogs whilest the Lyon held them both vnder his power, did byte the Lyon by the belly, whereat the Lyon roared so extreamely, that the earth shooke withall: and the next Lyon rampt and roared as if hee would haue made rescue....
>
> The two first dogs dyed within few dayes, but the last Dog was well recouered of all his hurts, & the yong Prince commaunded his seruant *Ed. Allen* to bring the dog to him to Saint *Iames,* where the Prince charged the sayd *Allen* to keepe him, and make much of him, saying, hee that had fought with the King of beasts, should neuer after fight with any inferiour creature.

That's entertainment.

Some years earlier the said Alleyn had shared a stage with a vision of Helen of Troy and delivered a speech that may be counted among the brightest plumes supplied by Marlowe:

> Was this the face that launched a thousand ships,
> And burnt the topless towers of Ilium?
> Sweet Helen, make me immortal with a kiss.
> Her lips suck forth my soul. See where it flies!
> Come, Helen, come, give me my soul again.
> Here will I dwell, for heaven is in these lips,
> And all is dross that is not Helena.

That's entertainment too.

The actor who had so often treated writers and other

lesser beings with a lord-of-the-manor style acquired the substance in 1605. Alleyn became Lord of the Manor of Dulwich when he bought that property for £5,000; he is supposed to have remarked that the price was "£1,000 more than any other man would have given for it." Additional acquisitions in the area cost another £5,000. At Dulwich Alleyn lived the life of a country gentleman; and on his fiftieth birthday, September 1, 1616, the chapel of the College of God's Gift was consecrated by no less a figure than the Archbishop of Canterbury.

And now it is time for a quiz.

*The two chief administrative officers of the College of God's Gift were the master and warden. Supply the last name of every master and warden from 1619 to 1857.*

I trust that none of you had any trouble with this. If you're confused, keep in mind that the answer reflects the ego of a superstar-mogul.

It is, of course, *Alleyn.* Among the statutes and ordinances that Alleyn put into place was one that directed that the master and warden must be "of my blood and surname," and also celibate. The Alleyns had no children, so only a few early masters and wardens could claim any kinship to the founder, but a long succession of Alleyns—along with a few Allens and one Alleyne (minor variations in spelling were permitted)—continued until the school was reorganized by an act of Parliament in the mid-nineteenth century.

The mechanism by which these Alleyns were selected was even stranger. Alleyn's statutes called for the warden to succeed the master when the post became vacant. A new warden was then chosen by this method: after the candidates were pared down to two, each drew a piece of paper to establish who would get the job.

Thus the school was run for more than two centuries by people whose credentials consisted of having the right name and a bit of luck. The author of a recent history of the school has noted that "this combination of demands made it almost impossible to find applicants of calibre: though some of the contestants were men of culture, over the centuries they formed a bizarre collection, including a vintner, peruke-maker, cooper, sea-captain, dyer, carpenter, grocer, timber-merchant, linen-merchant, hosier, malt-factor, and trooper."

The members of the college were also to be chosen by lot, and in Alleyn's day that provision brought forth the objection of a prominent educator, Dr. Nicholas Love, the headmaster of Winchester. But Alleyn did nothing to change the procedure; he obviously thought that he could bombast out a set of statutes and ordinances as well as the best of the educators.

# 7

## "...is in his own conceit..."

This is equivalent to "in his private opinion, estimation, or judgment," with an emphasis on something being supposed that is out of touch with reality. The *Oxford English Dictionary* includes examples from 1482—*Thys clerke ...was wise and wyttye in hys owne conceyte*—through 1704—*A drunkard does...fancy himself a king in his own conceit.* Shakespeare biographer Hazelton Spencer commented that it "means 'according to his own notions'; this phrase may reflect something Shakespeare had said or done." Honigmann suggested that Greene was pointing to "one who 'in his owne conceit' was the central figure in theatrical world." In 1592, of course, that was Alleyn.

## "...the only..."

Carrying the force of "the only one to be counted, reckoned, or considered."

## "...in a country..."

Equivalent to "in the country."

## "...the only shake-scene in a country."

With one additional twist, "shake" means "shake"; what

first demands our attention is "scene." In Greek the word *skene* means, among other things, "stage." Greek *skene* was taken into Latin as *scaena* and from there made its way into the Romance languages. One commentator has pointed to "Greene's interest in 'Englishing' words of Latin, Greek, French, and Italian origins." Elizabethans were rooted in the classics, and while they used "scene" to denote a subdivision of a play, it was also available as a synonym for "stage." Here, for example, is a remark found in a prologue to one of Ben Jonson's plays:

> The ends of all, who for the *Scene* doe write,
> Are, or should be, to profit, and delight.

Now for "shake." A theatrical scholar has noted that "the Elizabethan actor expected to find wooden boards under his feet, boards raised up off the ground, laid on trestles, on large hogshead barrels, or set on fixed posts. The boards must, therefore, have responded noisily to his feet." That would have been especially true for Alleyn, who was so renowned for a heavily physical style of acting that "stalking Tamburlaine" became an Elizabethan cliché. Here's a fanciful put-down line from a contemporary comedy that reflects the familiar image of Alleyn in full stride: "Dost stampe mad Tamberlaine, dost stampe? thou thinkst th'ast [bricks and] Morter vnder thy feete, dost?"

Among Alleyn's starring vehicles was *Tamar Cham*, a two-part play, now lost, highlighting the conquests of an Eastern potentate. While Jonson praised Alleyn publicly, in his journal he complained of "the *Tamerlanes*, and *Tamer-Chams* of the late Age, which had nothing in them but the *scenicall* strutting, and furious vociferation, to warrant them to the ignorant gapers." Another lost play that provided Alleyn with a starring role was *Cutlack*, and once again his footwork proved memorable—a satirist of the day made mention of "*Allens Cutlacks* gate [gait]." Alleyn's arm motions were equally forceful; there exists a description from 1597 of a person moving "vp and downe the rome [room], with such furious Iesture as if he had beene playing Tamberlane on a stage."

With Alleyn, though, there was shaking—and then there was *shaking.* A sense of "shake" exists carrying the force of "to cause (a structure) to totter; hence, to impair the stability of, to weaken." The *OED* includes this example from 1569: "And with his great artillary [he] sore battered and shaked the Walles." Before moving to the Rose in 1592 Alleyn's company performed at the Theatre in 1590 and 1591. Some years later, in 1604, Thomas Middleton described a "villainous" lieutenant as having "a head of hayre like one of [the] Diuells in Docter *Faustus*, when the olde Theater crackt and frighted the Audience."

*The English Wagner Book of 1594*, a translation and adaptation of a German account of Faustus and his servant Wagner, may provide specific evidence of what actually cracked that day. In the scene that Chambers has called "our nearest approach to a pen picture of an Elizabethan stage," Wagner brings forth a vision of Faustus in a theatrical performance. The play comes to an abrupt end "when *Faustus* hauing long raged...leapt down headlong of the stage, the whole company immediatly vanishing, but the stage, with a most monstrous thundering crack followed *Faustus* hastely, the people verily thinking they would haue fallen vppon them ran all away, and he was happiest that had the swiftest foote."

This account correlates with Middleton in significant respects—a Faustus performance, a crack, and the ensuing panic in the audience. Given Alleyn's reputation for making stages shake, it was exactly the sort of thing that an adversary would not allow him to forget.

## "...supposes he is...in his own conceit..."

The concept of *shaking a stage* was hardly unique to Greene. Jonson used it in one of the prefatory poems included in the First Folio when he compared Shakespeare to the great playwrights of antiquity and declared that he would call them

> To life againe, to heare thy Buskin tread,
> And shake a Stage.

Here the buskin—the boot used in performing tragedies—serves for the act of writing tragedies. Shakespeare was a far better playwright than he was an actor, but Greene's concerns with Alleyn are just the reverse—the superstar-mogul as bad writer.

An important indication as to why Greene needed "shake-scene" to convey his meaning can be found in the parallelism of *supposes he is* and *is in his own conceit*; it links the claim of being able to bombast out a blank verse to the pride of being a shake-scene, with both being viewed through the prism of Greene's sneer. The message is: what Alleyn does when he tinkers with the scene of a play is equivalent to what he did to the scene of the Theatre. To paraphrase: no one can bring down the house—or a play—like he can.

When a mogul fancies himself a writer the results, of course, are highly predictable. French novelist Romain Gary served a stint in Hollywood and came away deploring the fact that Darryl Zanuck liked to think of himself as a writer, "and he wrote like a pig, like a real pig, it was incredible what came out of his pen." Gary said, "He knows good writing in other people but not bad in himself....Just one touch of Darryl and it begins to stink."

One day Gary placed a banana on the table at the beginning of a meeting with Zanuck. When Zanuck asked the obvious question, Gary explained that the banana was there to remind him that he was dealing with a gorilla. Far from being taken aback by the remark, from that point on Zanuck provided a plate of bananas whenever he had a session with Gary.

Greene was facing the same sort of figure: ambitious, hard-driving (and driven), highly effective when he sticks to doing what he does best, and someone for whom animal imagery is altogether appropriate. But as for being a writer—recall that scene from the earlier part of *Groat's-worth* when the player regales Roberto with "a plaine rime extempore," promising, "If ye will ye shall haue more."

"Nay its enough," Roberto replied.

**"...the 'real' cause..."**

"The punning reference to a Shake-scene," Samuel Schoenbaum has commented, "and the parody of a line from *3 Henry VI*...identify the victim unmistakably. Less clear is the purport of the attack, couched as it is in obscurely allusive language"; but Schoenbaum suggested that Greene was sneering at an actor who has "set himself up as a universal genius (*Johannes fac totum*)" and has tried "to rival his betters by turning out plays in stilted blank verse." Yet Roland Mushat Frye, author of *Shakespeare: The Art of the Dramatist*, found the intent of Greene's attack to be clear enough. Frye commented that "shake-scene" was "a derogatory pun on the author's name, while the whole effect was to depict Shakespeare as a fellow of unjustified arrogance and pretentious incompetence."

For the Shakespeareans "shake-scene" is obviously a pun—unless it isn't. Alfred Harbage, who was for years a prominent member of the English department at Harvard, once wrote, "We can argue that 'Shake-scene' is a common type of epithet, like 'Tear-throat,' and might indicate *any* allegedly bombastic playwright, but in view of the other particularities in the passage (each individually vulnerable), the case for Shakespeare becomes too strong to be denied, and few are inclined to deny it."

If you look in the *Oxford English Dictionary* you'll find that "tear-throat" is defined as "a ranting actor," not playwright. The *OED* offers this example from 1654: "The Poets of the Fortune and red Bull, had alwayes a mouth-measure for their Actors (who were terrible teare throats)." Unlike the situation with the Fortune, Alleyn did not have a financial stake in the Red Bull, but he did note in his diary that he traveled to that playhouse on October 3, 1617, and sold the actors a play that he owned.

The importance of "shake-scene" to the Shakespearean position cannot be underestimated. The *Henry VI* authorship debate—still not settled after more than two centuries of controversy—effectively eliminates the usefulness of "tiger's heart" for the identification of Shakespeare as the upstart crow; and even if one were inclined to accept as fact the upstart crow's braggadocio of being able to bombast out a blank verse, it's worth remembering that there was nothing particularly remarkable about being an actor-playwright in this period—Tarlton was the author of *The Seven Deadly Sins*, and an actor named Robert Wilson wrote three plays in the 1580s and 1590s.

Yet for the Shakespeareans "shake-scene" is still hazy after all these years. T. W. Baldwin of the University of Illinois saw Greene as pointing to Shakespeare's lapses in failing to follow the neo-classical dictates of proper playwriting; what undoes this notion is that Greene freely ignored these rules in his own plays. Sigurd Burckhardt, formerly of The Ohio State University, decided to construct "a speculative little playlet" that he hoped would take in *Groat's-worth* and a theory on the authorship of *1 Henry VI* as well. Burckhardt viewed collaborative writing as "a practice which must have encouraged each playwright to try to be the best 'Shake-scene,' to outdo his colleagues and competitors in the writing of theatrically effective scenes and let the play as a whole shift for itself." If Shakespeare had become frustrated with this process and decided to complete the text on his own, he might appear to Greene and the other writers as someone who "arrogantly set himself up as the '*only* Shake-scene' (i.e., demanding to write *all* the scenes)."

Here "shake-scene" becomes a term that could be applied to *any* playwright of bombastic tendencies, but Burckhardt did not press the point to its logical conclusion—that there is nothing intrinsically Shakespearean about "shake-scene." He intended his view to serve as "a model, an interpretive device," that might be able to chart a parallel between the power struggles depicted in the play and the supposed battles within the ranks of the playwrights; and he offered as a conclusion that "it is unlikely that we will discover the 'real' cause of Greene's attack on Shakespeare and the players; but we may discover what Shakespeare 'made of it.' "

"Shake," of course, is a common verb that readily forms

compounds, and Elizabethan examples of "shake" constructions are not difficult to find. A 1592 play featured two bumbling criminals named Black Will and Shakebag, but only the rare commentator has attempted to discern in this a portrait of the artist as a young punk. Will Kemp, the comic actor who played Constable Dogberry in *Much Ado About Nothing*, chose to employ the contemptuous term "shake-rags" in addressing the ballad writers of the day; yet even though used by a colleague, the word has nothing to do with Shakespeare.

"Shake-scene" caught the attention of H. J. Oliver of the University of New South Wales. In Australian slang "shake" means "steal," and it once had that meaning in England. "Commentators and biographers seem content to refer vaguely to a 'pun,' " Oliver wrote, noting that they "apparently understand by this no more than that 'shake' is the first syllable of Greene's word and of 'Shakespeare.' The explanation is inadequate." Oliver, though, remained within the pale of orthodoxy as he set forth yet another version of the plagiarism theory: "Greene *was* probably accusing Shakespeare of *stealing* 'scenes' and was saying that Shakespeare believed himself to be the only dramatist clever enough to make plays from the work of others." But how clever would a writer have to be to do that?

Sometimes a "shake" is just a "shake."

# 8

GREENE'S ATTACK.
CHETTLE'S APOLOGY.
SHAKESPEARE'S REPLY.

Since attacks on writers generally produce in-print responses, this would seem to represent a logical progression in any Shakespearean view of *Groat's-worth*; yet Shakespeare's reply has remained an elusive quarry even for the most assiduous searchers.

Muriel Bradbrook observed that *Venus and Adonis*, the first of two narrative poems written by Shakespeare, was licensed only seven months after *Groat's-worth.* She found significance in the timing: "Shakespeare's first venture into print, while not a direct reply to Greene's *Groats-worth of Witte*, may be regarded as a response provoked by this piece of vilification." Nothing in *Venus and Adonis* speaks to Greene's attack on the upstart crow, but for Bradbrook that only serves as an indication that Shakespeare chose to write "not with the common style of disclaimer but with positive demonstration of new and dazzling capacities."

I suggest, however, that if any work is to be credited with playing a part in bringing forth *Venus and Adonis* it would be Marlowe's narrative poem *Hero and Leander*, which was then known in manuscript form. That would put Shakespeare in the position of matching Marlowe narrative poem for narrative poem, a calculation that can go a long way toward claiming both sequence and consequence.

Sonnet 112 made use of the fact that criminals who had received a brand would sometimes attempt to cover it over; and Shakespeare's phrasing has attracted the attention of those looking for a reply to *Groat's-worth*:

> Your loue and pittie doth th'impression fill,
> Which vulgar scandall stampt vpon my brow,
> For what care I who calles me well or ill,
> So you ore-greene my bad, my good alow?

Edgar I. Fripp commented in his biography of Shakespeare that "*o'er-greene* [Fripp's spelling] is surely a reply to *Shakescene*. It is a word coined for the purpose and never used again. Such play on proper names is common in the contemporary sonnet." Fripp's position found support from John Berryman, who wrote, "Though not much addicted to cryptograms, I feel the suggestion as plausible which sees in the otherwise unknown word 'o'er-greene' an allusion to the name of his tormentor, somewhat as in 'out-Herod,' the meaning of the clause then being: If you wipe out Greene's insult to what *is* ill in me, my occupation..."

This view, however, is not responsive to the thrust of Shakespeare's imagery. The *OED* defines "overgreen" as "to cover with green, clothe with verdure; hence *fig.*, to cover so as to conceal a defect, embellish"; and Stephen Booth remarks in his edition of the *Sonnets* that filling in a brand is "comparable to replacing divots in damaged turf." The concept is not one of *covering over* green, but covering over *with* green. The patch of green, therefore, is a palliative measure, not the source of the problem. Moreover, the roots of "overgreen" are not impossible to find.

In Edmund Spenser's *Shepherds Calendar* (1579) a

shepherd named Diggon speaks allegorically of those who abuse the church: "For they bene like foule wagmoires [quagmires] ouergrast." In the notes to the original edition "overgrassed" is glossed as "ouergrowen with grasse." To Diggon's statement another shepherd responds:

> Nowe Diggon, I see thou speakest to[o] plaine:
> Better it were, a little to feyne,
> And cleanly couer, that cannot be cured.
> Such il, as is forced, mought [must] nedes be endured.

Foul quagmires overgrassed; matters incurable cleanly covered; an ill that must be endured—all of this is to be found in a work by a highly-respected poet of the time.

The Nashe-Harvey dispute was one of the more celebrated literary diversions of the 1590s; it received much of its impetus from Greene's attack on the Harvey family in *A Quip for an Upstart Courtier.* Gabriel Harvey, a Cambridge academic who had acquired a law degree, went to London looking for justice, but suffered the disappointment of learning that his enemy had only recently died. Harvey then put pen to paper, producing a series of letters filled with outraged and rancorous accounts of Greene's life in the capital. These outpourings were brought into print by a publisher named John Wolfe, and while no one but a typesetter would want to justify everything Harvey wrote, paradoxically he remains among our best sources of information about Greene. Harvey's diatribe moved Nashe to enter the booksellers' lists, in part as a defender of Greene but also as a free-lance satirist who had found a target of opportunity.

*Love's Labour's Lost* is Shakespeare's most topical play, and there are indications that it includes references to this war of words. In the view of Richard David, the New Arden editor, "Gabriel Harvey's favourite style" is reflected in an overwrought love letter composed by the play's resident windbag, the Spaniard Don Adriano de Armado. Armado has a page named Moth whom he terms "my tender juvenal," an earlier form of "juvenile." That could lead one to think of *Groat's-worth*'s "young Juvenal," and the allusion is strengthened by puns on purses and pennies, reminiscent of the title of one of Nashe's best-known books, *Pierce Penniless.* (Elizabethans pronounced "pierce" as "purse.") That has led David to conclude, "Moth, therefore, here is Nashe."

In their Cambridge edition Sir Arthur Quiller-Couch and John Dover Wilson noted that Nashe's distinctive style is "excellently parodied in Moth's longest speech," creating the "conviction that Moth is here speaking as Thomas Nashe—that the total is *aut Nashe aut nullus*" (either Nashe or no one). Yet Dover Wilson put forth an additional view that ought to have produced some difficulties for an upholder of *Groat's-worth* orthodoxy: he commented that the portrait of Nashe "is rather complimentary than otherwise. Had the original recognized it on the stage he might have felt flattered. For he is represented as an ally." Here is Nashe, closely associated with Greene; there is Greene, cast by the Shakespeareans in the role of Shakespeare's attacker; and the result is, for Dover Wilson, that Nashe is Shakespeare's ally.

In fact, the only way that Shakespeare's outlook on the Nashe-Harvey dispute becomes understandable is for him to have had no special interest in Greene. That would account for his finding the nimble-witted Nashe a more attractive figure than the pompous Harvey, and it would also explain why *Love's Labour's Lost* has only weak and tentative references to Greene.

Armado informs Moth that "green indeed is the color of lovers," and David comments in his notes that "there may well be a pun here on Robert Greene." When Moth speaks of "my penny of observation," the editor points to "the similar expression" in *Groat's-worth*, but there's not much there for a reply to Greene. A contemporary proverb held that "the penny is well spent that saves a groat." Imagine, if you will, what Shakespeare could have done with pennies and groats had he wanted to.

In *A Midsummer Night's Dream* Theseus reviews various possibilities for an evening's entertainment:

> "The thrice three Muses mourning for the death
> Of learning, late deceas'd in beggary?"
> That is some satire, keen and critical,
> Not sorting with a nuptial ceremony.

Charles Knight, a nineteenth-century Shakespeare biographer, thought that this remark could refer to Greene, and he was seconded in that view by James Orchard Halliwell. Halliwell, though, assured his readers that Shakespeare's halo was firmly in place:

> There is nothing in the consideration that the poet had been attacked by Greene as the "upstart crow," to render Mr. Knight's theory improbable. The allusion in the comedy, if applicable to Greene, was certainly not conceived in an unkind spirit; and the death of one who at most was probably rather jealous than bitterly inimical, under such afflicting circumstances, there can be no doubt would have obliterated all trace of animosity from a mind so generous as was that of Shakespeare.

More recently A. L. Rowse has commented of the passage, "This is fairly clearly a reference to Greene's recent death in 1592; it is respectfully phrased." If Greene is indeed being referred to here—and it is far from clear that he is—this sort of respectful yet disengaged commentary could only come from someone who had no involvement with the *Groat's-worth* controversy.

Greene's *Orlando Furioso* has a scene in which the title character discovers love poetry hanging on the limbs of trees; he also delivers a speech to Venus as the Fair Queen of Love and the morning and evening star. In *As You Like It* the character that Shakespeare named Orlando celebrates his love for Rosalind by placing love poetry on the limbs of trees as he calls upon the aid of Diana, the moon goddess.

Quiller-Couch and Dover Wilson have noted, "These coincidences, which can hardly be accidental, establish a connexion of some sort or other between the two plays." Whatever that may be, it's clear that encountering the verses of her admirer has the effect of making Rosalind more delightful than ever. While initially complaining of a "tedious homily of love," she soon demands to know from her friend Celia: "What did he when thou saw'st him? What said he? How looked he? Wherein went he? What makes he here? Did he ask for me? Where remains he? How parted he with thee? And when shalt thou see him again? Answer me in one word." One would be hard pressed to believe that the stage device that set this into motion had been borrowed from Shakespeare's bitterest enemy.

In the second act of *Hamlet* Polonius reads a letter written by Hamlet "to the celestial and my soul's idol, the most beautified Ophelia." He then adds a response of his own: "That's an ill phrase, a vile phrase, 'beautified' is a vile phrase."

Bradbrook found a special meaning in Polonius' remark. While praising Shakespeare's "notable exercise of reason and self-control" by avoiding an in-print quarrel over *Groat's-worth,* she commented that "it must be assumed...that the attack cut deep. Years after, Polonius remembered that 'beautified' is a vile word." Another commentator, G. M. Pinciss, showed more caution on this point, writing that Shakespeare inserted the response "possibly as a gloss on Greene's words." Pinciss, however, pointed to Shakespeare's industriousness to explain his lack of interest in responding to *Groat's-worth*: "Even had Greene lived, the Stratford upstart was too busy writing successful plays to indulge in the sports of a Thomas Nashe or a Gabriel Harvey."

But Harold Jenkins, editor of the New Arden *Hamlet,* made no reference to *Groat's-worth* in his extended note on "beautified." He observed that the term had a legitimate existence in ornate Elizabethan prose—in 1593 Nashe composed a dedication "To the Most Honored, and Vertvovs [virtuous] Beavtified Ladie, The Ladie *Elizabeth Carey*"—and Jenkins concluded that such usages "forbid us to regard Hamlet's superscription as wildly extravagant; and though Shakespeare sees it to be vulnerable, by subjecting it to Polonius's criticism he to some degree protects it from our own."

The most readily discernible link between Shakespeare and Greene comes with one of Shakespeare's late plays, *The Winter's Tale.* Fitzroy Pyle, author of a book-length study of the play, has commented, "We are, it seems to me, obliged to take source material into account, especially when, as in the case of *The Winter's Tale,* a single book stands out as having been the constant object of the writer's attention in the act of composition." That book was *Pandosto: The Triumph of Time*, one of Greene's best-known prose fictions. Among the changes Shakespeare made was to add a happy—if improbable—ending.

Shakespeare also bestowed the name Mamillius on the young prince; this is the masculine form of Mamillia, the title character of Greene's first published work. Moreover, when the action of the play shifts to Bohemia—and, yes, it was Greene who provided Bohemia with a coast—a rogue named Autolycus displays pickpocketing techniques that closely reflect Greene's accounts of the London cony-catchers. In a book on Shakespeare's sources Kenneth Muir has commented, "It is curious that Shakespeare should be able to combine in a single play the two totally different kinds of work written by Greene—the romantic, unrealistic novel and the sordid documentaries of the seamy side of Elizabethan London."

Curious indeed—because even as it is clear that Greene was very much on Shakespeare's mind as he was writing *The Winter's Tale,* there is no indication that the blast against the upstart crow possessed any significance for him. The play contains no direct response, nor does it hold sly innuendos or verbal winks to the knowing. As an editor of the play has commented, "Shakespeare seems to have calmly ignored" Greene's attack.

# *Epilogue*

THERE'S AN OLD JOKE DATING BACK TO THE DAYS WHEN THE south side of Columbus was a haven for German immigrants; to make sense of it you need to know that bock beer is brewed in the spring.

Here's how it goes: a guy walks into a saloon and announces that he's selling Shakespeare. The saloonkeeper shakes his head and replies, "Well, we have Hoster's beer, and we have Born's beer, and we have Schlee's beer, but I never heard of this Shakespeare."

"No, no," says the man. "It's a book."

"Ah," says the saloonkeeper. "You come back in the springtime. Then we have the book beer."

You'll note that I didn't say this joke was *funny*—only that it was old. But in its own way it makes the point that we tend to view the world in terms of our major interests.

*Groat's-worth* has been used by the Shakespeare biographers as a source to locate materials on Shakespeare's arrival on the London theatre scene. As a result, Greene's attack on the upstart crow has ceased to convey a discernible, comprehensible meaning. The biographers remain unconcerned; at the center of their world is Shakespeare.

But Greene *does* matter. The attack on the upstart crow is impassioned; the writing is fluid, even elegant; and the sum of Greene's anger and frustration cannot simply be debited to the account of some strange neurotic envy.

To read Greene as if Greene matters is, to be sure, a radical measure, as it involves replanting these outpourings within the soiled confines of an entertainment business marked by the overarchings of a dominating ego; but until the Shakespeare scholars and biographers are willing to make such a commitment, their understanding of *Groat's-worth* must forever remain inadequate.

# *Notes*

**Page 7** *"Yes trust them"*: Robert Greene, *Groats-vvorth of Witte, bought with a million of Repentance,* ed. G. B. Harrison, with *The Repentance of Robert Greene, 1592,* The Bodley Head Quartos (New York: E. P. Dutton, 1923), pp. 45-46. See also Thomas W. Cobb, "A Critical Edition of Robert Greene's *Groatsworth of Wit,*" 2 vols. (Ph.D. dissertation, Yale University, 1977), 2: 51-52.

*The equivalent of italics*: *Groat's-worth* was printed in black letter (the font that is popularly known as Old English). In a black-letter text Roman type functions in the role of italics.

**Page 8** *"There can be"*: *The Plays of William Shakespeare: in Ten Volumes; with the Corrections and Illustrations of Various Commentators; to Which Are Added Notes by Samuel Johnson and George Steevens,* ed. George Steevens, 2d ed., rev. and augmented, 10 vols. (London: C. Bathurst et al., 1778), 6: 566.

*"Of uncertain"*: *Oxford English Dictionary*, s.v. "shakescene."

**Page 9** *"The passage is ambiguous"*: F. E. Halliday, *Shakespeare and His Critics* (London: Duckworth, 1949), p. 30.

*"The Norwich blaggard"*: Review of *William Shakespeare: A Documentary Life*, by S. Schoenbaum, *Eastern Daily Press*, April 28, 1975.

*"O tiger's heart"*: *3 Henry VI*, 1.4.137.

**Page 10** *"Bred a stage-player"*: Thomas Fuller, *The Worthies of England*, ed. John Freeman (London: George Allen & Unwin, 1952), p. 368.

**Page 11** *"This attack"*: Isaac Disraeli, *Amenities of Literature, Consisting of Sketches and Characters of English Literature*, new ed., ed. Benjamin Disraeli, 2 vols. (New York: A. C. Armstrong and Son, 1880), 2: 194. *"Shakespeare's actual role"*: C. L. Barber and Richard P. Wheeler, *The Whole Journey: Shakespeare's Power of Development* (Berkeley: University of California Press, 1986), p. 61. The book was begun by Barber and completed after his death by Wheeler.

**Page 12** *"The ignorant monster"*: M. C. Bradbrook, *Shakespeare the Craftsman* (London: Chatto & Windus, 1969), p. 15.

*"A perfectly normal"*: J. Dover Wilson, "Malone and the Upstart Crow," *Shakespeare Survey 4* (Cambridge: Cambridge University Press, 1951), p. 62.

*"In the whole"*: Peter Alexander, *Shakespeare's* Henry VI *and* Richard III (Cambridge: Cambridge University Press, 1929), pp. 45-46.

**Page 13** *"Greene was"*: Gareth Lloyd Evans, *The Upstart Crow: An Introduction to Shakespeare's Plays*, ed. and rev. Barbara Lloyd Evans (London: J. M. Dent & Sons, 1982), p. v.

*"The vital significance"*: John Semple Smart, *Shakespeare: Truth and Tradition* (London: Edward Arnold, 1928), pp. 195-96.

**Page 14** *"Probably used"*: Eric Partridge, *A Dictionary of Catch Phrases, British and American, from the Sixteenth Century to the Present Day* (London: Routledge & Kegan Paul, 1977), p. 234.

*"Pretentious," "criticism," "This passage"*: Smart, *Truth and Tradition*, pp. 194, 196.

*"One can sympathize"*: S. Schoenbaum, *William Shakespeare: A Documentary Life* (Oxford: Clarendon Press, 1975), p. 119.

**Page 15** *"As for the vision"*: The remark was made by William Kelley in his acceptance speech at the Academy Awards presentation on March 24, 1986. He was one of three winners for the screenplay of *Witness.*

*The screenplay of* Casablanca: Ian Hamilton, *Writers in Hollywood, 1915-1951* (New York: Harper & Row, 1990), pp. 242-45.

*"In comes* Chettle": *Thomas Dekker's* A Knights Conjuring *(1607): A Critical Edition*, ed. Larry M. Robbins (The Hague: Mouton, 1974), p. 157.

*"Vppon the perill"*: *A Transcript of the Registers of the Company of Stationers of London; 1554-1640 A.D.*, ed. Edward Arber, 4 vols. (London: privately published, 1875), 2:620.

*"Letter written" and other quotations from Chettle in this chapter*: Henry Chettle, *Kind-Hartes Dreame, 1592*, with William Kemp, *Nine Daies Wonder, 1600*, ed. G. B. Harrison, The Bodley Head Quartos (London: John Lane, The Bodley Head, 1923), pp. 5-6, 13. The possibility that Chettle did more than copy the text of *Groat's-worth,* that he wrote it himself, was raised by Chauncey Sanders in "Robert Greene and His 'Editors,'" *PMLA*, 48(1933): 392-417. Sanders was answered by Harold Jenkins in "On the Authenticity of *Greene's Groatsworth of Wit* and *The Repentance of Robert Greene*," *Review of English Studies*, 11(1935): 28-41. There the matter rested until 1969 when Warren B. Austin employed an entirely different technique to make the case for Chettle's authorship. Austin fed into a computer samples of Greene's and Chettle's writings and arrived at the conclusion that "the patterns of

language habit and preference disclosed by a multi-variable analysis of this purported last book of Greene's are far different from those characteristic of his style; and they match very closely those Chettle consistently exhibited in his known writings." For Austin this set of results "resoundingly confirms the hypothesis that the book was a literary forgery by Chettle." Yet he was forced to credit Chettle with "a *tour de force* of literary impersonation" to overcome the objection that "to many, its poignant personal revelations have carried such a ring of truth as to make forgery unthinkable" (Warren B. Austin, *A Computer-Aided Technique for Stylistic Discrimination: The Authorship of* Greene's Groatsworth of Wit [U.S. Department of Health, Education, and Welfare, 1969], pp. 78, 74). While Austin pointed to *Kind-Heart's Dream* as an example of Chettle's ability to assume a role in print, I find that material to be a tepid formulation when set alongside the sharply resonating complaint against the upstart crow. In a review for *Shakespeare Quarterly* Ruth L. Widmann commented that Austin's analysis was "ultimately unconvincing" (23 [1972]: 215); and T. R. Waldo, writing in *Computers and the Humanities*, concluded that Austin's "technique is inconclusive" when applied to *Groat's-worth* (7 [1972]: 110).

**Page 17** *"Famous as well"*: Sir Richard Baker, *Theatrum Redivivum, or the Theatre Vindicated* (orig. ed., 1662; reprint ed., New York: Johnson Reprint Corp., 1972), p. 48 (D8$^{v}$). *"A very shrewd"*: John Briley, "Edward Alleyn and Henslowe's Will," *Shakespeare Quarterly*, 9(1958): 327.

*"This is"*: A. L. Rowse, *Shakespeare the Man* (London: Macmillan, 1973), p. 62. *"May have been"*: Peter Quennell, *Shakespeare: A Biography* (Cleveland: World Publishing, 1963), p. 64. Quennell thought that the Earl of Southampton might have been included in the "divers of worship," but the proper mode of address for a member of the nobility would have been "of honor," not "of worship." William A. Ringler, Jr., noted that the distinction "was scrupulously observed in Elizabethan times"; thus Chettle "was clearly referring to the reports of gentlemen only" ("Spenser, Shakespeare, Honor, and Worship," *Renaissance News*, 14 [1961]: 161). *"The apology"*: T. W. Baldwin, *On the Literary Genetics of Shakspere's Plays, 1592-1594* (Urbana, Ill.: University of Illinois Press, 1959), p. 54.

*"Something disingenuous"*: M. M. Reese, *Shakespeare: His World and His Work*, rev. ed. (London: Edward Arnold, 1983), p. 136.

**Page 18** *On the "lost years"*: On May 6, 1593, the Privy Council in London issued a special license to "Edward Allen, servaunt to the right honorable the Lord Highe Admiral, William Kemp, Thomas Pope, John Heminges, Augustine Phillipes and Georg Brian, being al one companie, servauntes to our verie good the Lord the Lord Straingе" (E. K. Chambers, *The Elizabethan Stage*, 4 vols. [Oxford: Clarendon Press, 1923], 2:123). Shakespeare is prominent by his absence. If he were in the company he may have chosen not to go on tour, or he may not have been prominent enough to warrant notice by officialdom. Of course, the answer may well be that he was not a member of the company at this time.

An internal document created by Strange's men, the prompter's plot for the second part of *The Seven Deadly Sins*, failed to include Shakespeare although it does have a non-speaking part not assigned to a specific actor. It is possible, if one wants to make the speculation, to make up for the prompter's laxness and assign the part to Shakespeare. The plot includes a boy named Will, no last name given. E. A. J. Honigmann chose to make the point that "women were sometimes acted by fairly mature 'boys' in their late teens; Shakespeare would have been 26 in 1590" (*Shakespeare: The "Lost Years"* [Manchester: Manchester University Press, 1985], p. 59).

In 1594 Lord Strange died and the company acquired a new patron in the Lord Chamberlain. Following a ten-day stint in a suburban playhouse the amalgamation with Alleyn came to an end. The Chamberlain's men performed at court that December, and on March 15, 1595, payment was made to "William Kempe William Shakespeare & Richarde Burbage seruantes to the Lord Chamberleyne" (E. K. Chambers, *William Shakespeare: A Study of Facts and Problems*, 2 vols. [Oxford: Clarendon Press, 1930], 2:319). This sort of unequivocal evidence placing Shakespeare in the Chamberlain's men is lacking when it comes to showing an involvement with Strange's men.

As far as the writing of the plays is concerned, Chambers set forth a chronology that put *2* and *3 Henry VI* in 1590-91, *1 Henry VI* in 1591-92, *Richard III* and *The Comedy of Errors* in 1592-93, and *Titus Andronicus* and *The Taming of the Shrew* in 1593-94 (ibid., 1:270). As with *2* and *3 Henry VI, 1 Henry VI* has come under discussion for its authorship. Gary Taylor made a different set of choices for the new Oxford edition, placing the beginning of Shakespeare's career with *The Two Gentlemen of Verona* and *The Taming of the Shrew* in 1590-91, *2* and *3 Henry VI* in 1591, *1 Henry VI* and *Titus Andronicus* in 1592, and *Richard III* in 1592-93 ("The Canon and Chronology of Shakespeare's Plays," in *William Shakespeare: A Textual Companion*, ed. Stanley Wells and Gary Taylor with John Jowett and William Montgomery [Oxford: Clarendon Press, 1987], pp. 109-16).

Honigmann, however, has argued for a much earlier dating of the beginning of Shakespeare's career. In his view Shakespeare was not only a member of Strange's men but also "enjoyed a very special *social* position in Lord Strange's circle, and that could explain why Greene singled him out, maliciously, as the central figure amongst 'those puppets.'" Honigmann found it "relevant" that Greene dedicated a book in 1584 to Lord Strange's mother and another in 1589 to Lord Strange (*"Lost Years,"* pp. 70, 71). This position, however, bestows a significance where none actually exists; in his constant quest for a patron Greene composed a multitude of dedications and those rank as merely two among many.

Shakespeare may well have started to write for the theatre before Greene died; but considering that in the Letter to the Playwrights Greene could overlook so important a figure as Kyd, there is no reason to believe that he would have felt obliged to concern himself with a playwright newly arrived on the scene.

*"Biographers are"*: Russell Fraser, *Young Shakespeare* (New York: Columbia University Press, 1988), p. 145.

*"These two references"*: John Dover Wilson, *The Essential Shakespeare: A Biographical Adventure* (Cambridge: Cambridge University Press, 1932), p. 45.

**Page 19** *C. S. Lewis has done so*: *Studies in Words* (Cambridge: Cambridge University Press, 1960), pp. 86-110.

*"An old groat" and other quotations from* Groat's-worth *in this chapter*: *Groats-vvorth of Witte,* ed. Harrison, pp. 10, 33-34, 36, 39.

**Page 20** *"To build a Windmill"*: On the player's claim Cobb suggests, "Act ambitiously or misguidedly (?), create a setting for performing plays with windy rhetoric or bombast (?)" ("Critical Edition," 2:37a). On "footback" see *The Works of Thomas Nashe*, ed. Ronald B. McKerrow, 5 vols. (orig. ed., 1904-10; reprint ed., Oxford: Basil Blackwell, 1958), 4:458. Nashe used the term in his preface to Greene's *Menaphon* (see below).

M. C. Bradbrook has commented that this player "sounds as if it could be Shakespeare; the Burbages and Alleyn were not countrymen" (*Shakespeare: The Poet in His World* [New York: Columbia University Press, 1978], p. 50). But Alleyn toured the countryside and, as with the player, would have found himself alone in being impressed by his writing abilities. Alleyn, of course, also hired writers.

A. L. Rowse has noted that the player's mention of a seven-year apprenticeship fits the period between the birth of Shakespeare's twins in 1585 and the publication of *Groat's-worth* in 1592 (*Shakespeare the Man*, p. 60). The player who hired Roberto, however, was not coming fresh from an apprenticeship; he was at the time well established in his profession.

*"Famous for Delphrigus"*: In his preface to *Menaphon*, a prose fiction by Greene published in 1589, Nashe pointed to writers who have "tricked vp a company of taffaty fooles with their feathers." Without their contribution actors "might haue antickt it vntill this time vp and downe the Countrey with the King of Fairies, and dined euery day at the pease porredge ordinary"—the Elizabethan equivalent of a greasy spoon—"with *Delfrigus*." Actors, Nashe warned, should be careful "lest their increasing indignities returne them ere long to their iugling to mediocrity, and they bewaile in weeping blankes [blank verse] the wane of their Monarchie" (*Nashe*, ed. McKerrow, 3: 323-24).

**Page 22** *"There was no more faith"*: *The Life and Complete Works in Prose and Verse of Robert Greene, M.A., Cambridge and Oxford*, ed. Alexander B. Grosart, 15 vols. [orig. ed., 1881-86; reprint ed., New York: Russell & Russell, 1964], 11: 76. This was included in *The Defense of Cony-Catching,* a pamphlet attributed on its title page to one Cuthbert Cony-Catcher. ("Cony" was the ordinary Elizabethan word for "rabbit" but in the criminals' argot it denoted a victim.) As befits a cony-catcher, the *comedians-chameleons* imagery was not original with Cuthbert. Chambers supplies an example from 1580 (*Stage*, 2: 98).

Most commentators—and I would agree—have viewed the *Defense* as an extension of Greene's cony-catching pamphlets and have attributed all or a substantial amount of the authorship to Greene himself. Cuthbert slyly remarks, "I found our art so perfectly anotomized, as if he [Greene] had bene practitioner in our facultie forty winters before" (*Greene,* ed. Grosart, 11: 45-46); and indeed, Greene's first cony-catching volume, *A Notable Discovery of Cozenage* (1591), includes passages lifted from Gilbert Walker's *A Manifest Detection of Diceplay* (1552), an earlier work purporting to chronicle the ways of criminals.

A dissenting view on Greene's authorship of the *Defense* has been put forth by I. A. Shapiro, who argued that "the denunciation of the double sale of *Orlando Furioso* is clear evidence that Greene did not write *The Defence*" ("An Unsuspected Earlier Edition of *The Defence of Conny-catching*," *The Library,* 5th ser., 18 [1963]: 111.) Yet when the most prominent actor in London's leading company was defrauded by a famous writer, word would be certain to get around; and since Greene was clearly in the wrong, a straightforward defense would not have accrued to his benefit. As a shrewd piece of gamesmanship playing on the writers' resentment of Alleyn the *Defense* constitutes an effective response to what Greene chose to see as the far greater outrages perpetrated by the actors. While it is true, as Shapiro points out, that no advantage would accrue to Greene if additional copies of the first two volumes of the cony-catching pamphlets were sold, the *Defense* was itself a sale to a publisher and Greene may well have expected increased demand for additional volumes in the series. Besides, in this sort of exercise, somewhere between a *jeu d'esprit* and a hoax, calculations of a strictly financial sort are not likely to be particularly helpful in assessing motivation. For a response to Shapiro see David Parker, "Robert Greene and *The Defence of Conny Catching*," *Notes and Queries*, n.s., 21 (1974): 87-89.

*"Fellas"*: Steven Bach, *Final Cut: Dreams and Disaster in the Making of* Heaven's Gate (New York: William Morrow, 1985), p. 70.

**Page 24** *Took up residence with a prostitute*: Gabriel Harvey claimed that Cutting Ball, who was ultimately hanged at Tyburn, provided Greene with bodyguards. Harvey also mentioned Greene's "keping of the foresaid Balls sister, a sorry ragged queane, of whome hee had his base sonne, *Infortunatus Greene*" (Gabriel Harvey, *Fovre Letters and certeine Sonnets, especially touching Robert Greene and other parties by him abused, 1592*, ed. G. B. Harrison, The Bodley Head Quartos [London: John Lane, The Bodley Head, 1922], p. 20). In assessing Greene's misdeeds, Harvey assured his readers that "particulars are infinite," but he was editorializing with the name of the son. Fortunatus Greene was buried on August 12, 1593, in Shoreditch. In telling Roberto's story Greene wrote, "The shamefull ende of sundry his consorts deseruedly punished for their amisse, wrought no compunction in his heart: of which one, brother to a Brothell [prostitute] hee kept, was trust [trussed] vnder a tree as round as a Ball" (*Groats-vvorth of Witte*, ed. Harrison, p. 37).

*A sleeved cloak*: This is mentioned by Nashe in *Strange News* (*Nashe*, ed. McKerrow, 1:288). Nashe was challenging Harvey's view of "the lowsie circumstance" of Greene's poverty (p. 287).

**Page 25** *"Spend their wits" and other quotations from* Groat's-worth *in this chapter*: *Groats-vvorth of Witte*, ed. Harrison, pp. 43, 44, 45, 46.

*On the second playwright*: The identity of this writer is the only one of the three that is open to some debate. Thomas Lodge wrote a play with Greene, *A Looking Glass for London and England*, and it was given one performance by Alleyn's company in 1592. It was, however, an old play by that time. If "lastly" were taken to mean "the last thing we wrote together," *Looking Glass* might qualify in that respect, although a separate issue would remain over whether it could be described as a comedy. While possessing some comic elements, the play has a strongly sermonizing tone. The case for Lodge as the second playwright can be found in Philip Drew, "Was Greene's 'Young Juvenal' Nashe or Lodge?" *Studies in English Literature*, 7 (1967): 55-66. I favor taking "lastly" to mean "recently"; this passage is included as an example in the *OED* under that definition. It has been suggested that "comedy" could refer to *The Defense of Cony-Catching* (see Charles Nicholl, *A Cup of News: The Life of Thomas Nashe* [London: Routledge & Kegan Paul, 1984], pp. 125-30), but Greene's quarrel with actors in the Letter to the Playwrights would make it more likely that he is referring to a play. It's also worth noting that Lodge was a member of the Cavendish expedition to South America at the time Greene was writing *Groat's-worth.* Greene makes reference to "two more, that both haue writ against" the actors (*Groats-vvorth*, ed. Harrison, p. 46), and if Lodge has a place in *Groat's-worth* it is much more likely to be there. In a 1589 book Lodge had included a vow not to

tie my pen to *Pennie-knaues* delight,
But live with fame, and so for fame to wright.

(*Scillaes Metamorphosis: Enterlaced with the vnfortunate loue of Glaucus* [London: Richard Jones, 1589], C4$^{v}$.) Whether or not this was a serious promise, Lodge did leave writing and became a physician.

**Page 26** *"Keep that bastard"*: Gary Carey attributes this to Louis B. Mayer (*All the Stars in Heaven: Louis B. Mayer's M-G-M* [New York: E. P. Dutton, 1981], p. 184).

**Page 27** *"We do not know"*: Dover Wilson, "Malone," pp. 63, 64.

*"I shall never"*: Joseph L. Mankiewicz and Gary Carey, *More About* All About Eve (New York: Random House, 1972), pp. 247-48.

*"Listen, Nunnally"*: Aaron Latham, *Crazy Sundays: F. Scott Fitzgerald in Hollywood* (New York: Viking Press, 1971), p. 173. Johnson rejected Fitzgerald's advice.

**Page 29** *"These gentlemen"*: *OED*, s.v. "upstart." *"Proud and vnmannerly"*: *Greene*, ed. Grosart, 11:223, 294.

*"So hautie"*: Christopher Marlowe, *Edward II*, ed. H. B. Charlton and R. D. Waller (London: Methuen, 1933), p. 147n. *"Pernitious upstarts," "Think you"*: *Edward II*, 3.1.165, 1.4.41.

**Page 30** *"Upstart"*: *1 Henry VI*, 4.7.88. *"Overbearing"*: *The First Part of King Henry VI*, ed. Andrew S. Cairncross, The [New] Arden Shakespeare (London: Methuen, 1962), p. 107n.

*On the Townley claim*: See Chambers, *Stage*, 2:296.

*"My good sweett mouse"*: *Henslowe Papers: Being Documents Supplementary to Henslowe's Diary*, ed. Walter W. Greg (orig. ed., 1907; reprint ed., New York: AMS Press, 1975), p. 35.

**Page 31** *"Comon curtesie" and other quotations from the letter*: Baird W. Whitlock, "Y$^{e}$ Curioust Schooler in Cristendom," *Review of English Studies*, n.s., 6(1955): 367, 368-69.

**Page 32** *"Both he"*: R. C. Bald, *John Donne: A Life* (New York: Oxford University Press, 1970), p. 466.

*"They are not your works"*: *The Sermons of John Donne*, ed. Evelyn M. Simpson and George R. Potter, 10 vols. (Berkeley and Los Angeles: University of California Press, 1953-62), 10:95-96. Whitlock is incorrect in his statement that Evelyn Simpson "shows that 1624/5 is the probable date" for Sermon 8 of the *LXXX Sermons* ("Curioust," p. 371). Simpson was unable to assign a date (*A Study of the Prose Works of John Donne*, 2d ed. [Oxford: Clarendon Press, 1948], p. 356).

*"Men of great honor"*: *Greene*, ed. Grosart, 8:131, 132.

**Page 33** *Source material*: See Macrobius, *The Saturnalia*, trans. Percival Vaughan Davies (New York: Columbia University Press, 1969), pp. 174-75, 233.

*"Roscius here"*: Schoenbaum, *Documentary Life*, p. 116. *"Greene uses"*: Peter Alexander, *Shakespeare* (London: Oxford University Press, 1964), p. 68.

**Page 34** *"It is admitted"*: William Young, *The History of Dulwich College...with a Life of the Founder, Edward Alleyn, and an Accurate Transcript of His Diary, 1617-1622*, 2 vols. (London: T. B. Bumpus, 1889), 1:vi.

*On Greene's plays*: Chambers thought that *Friar Bacon and Friar Bungay* was owned by Henslowe (*Stage*, 3:329). The Admiral's men offered a revival of a *Mahomet* in the summer of 1594, which may well have been Greene's *Alphonsus of Aragon.* Chambers noted that the company bought the book from Alleyn in 1601 (p. 327).

**Page 35** *"Any one playe"*: *Henslowe Papers*, ed. Greg, pp. 32, 33. *"Come, give us"*: *Hamlet*, 2.2.427-28.

**Page 36** *Dover Wilson's citing*: Dover Wilson commented that "Horace's crow and Aesop's were so closely associated in readers' minds in Shakespeare's day as to be practically identical" ("Malone," p. 65). But Horace's crow was not always used by Elizabethans in the context of plagiarism. In his 1585 edition of *Aesop's Fables* William Bullokar noted that Horace "teleth this fabl of a sely [silly] crow. He sayeth, that the crow being dekt with fetherz being gathered-toogether, which had fal'n from birds, was a moking-stok [mockingstock], after that eueryon of the birds had pluckt-of hiz fether" (*Æsops Fablz in tru Ortography with Grammar-nots* [London: Edmund Bollifant, 1585], D4$^{r}$). Here Horace's bird has become a mere adjunct to Aesop's. Since Greene plagiarized freely from other writers and even borrowed from his own work, for the upstart crow to receive his censure on this score the amount of literary borrowing would have had to have been so great that some clear evidence could be expected to have been left behind.

Andrew Cairncross thought he found an example in "Abradas, the great Masadonian Pyrate," a name that appears in the quarto of *2 Henry*

*VI* and was also used by Greene in two books. The Folio replaces it with "Bargulus the strong Illyrian pirate." Yet Cairncross had to conclude that if this can be considered a response to the attack in *Groat's-worth*, "then the plumes that Shakespeare recognized as borrowed from Greene must have been very few indeed" (*The Second Part of King Henry VI*, ed. Andrew S. Cairncross, The [New] Arden Shakespeare [London: Methuen, 1957], p. xliv). Cairncross also included in his argument Shakespeare's verbal echoings of classical writers; but his remarks earned the stricture of G. Blakemore Evans: "I do not find this interpretation of Greene's attack very persuasive. Why, one wonders, did Greene bother to raise his voice against Shakespeare on such a score as this?" (Review of *The Second Part of King Henry VI*, ed. Cairncross, *Shakespeare Quarterly*, 9 [1958]: 62).

*"A mere variation"*: Chambers, *Shakespeare*, 1:217. *"The phrase," "a pathetic document"*: Alexander, *Shakespeare's* Henry VI, pp. 44, 42-43.

**Page 37** *"The tiger"*: George Pettie, *A Petite Pallace of Pettie His Pleasure*, ed. Herbert Hartman (Oxford: Clarendon Press, 1938), p. 119. Chaucer used this conception of the tiger in "The Squire's Tale": "This tigre, ful of doublenesse" (l. 543).

*"The Tyger then hideth"*: *Greene*, ed. Grosart, 2:28. Greene made use of this formulation a second time; see Grosart, 9:66. *"When the Tygre"*: Ibid., 8:87. *"Well, trust him not"*: *Wily Begvilde* (London: Clement Knight, 1606), p. 44, F3$^{v}$. W. W. Greg has suggested "a date not long after 1596" for the play (The Malone Society Reprints, 1912, p. vii), while Chambers has commented that "the right date may be *c.* 1602-6" (*Stage*, 4:53).

Leslie Hotson included a collection of tiger quotations in *Shakespeare by Hilliard* (Berkeley and Los Angeles: University of California Press, 1977), pp. 143-45. Among these is a 1587 commentary from William Rankins concerning actors who, in proclaiming that "they hate harmes," only manage to "deceiue themselues, more unnaturall then the cruell Tygre" (*A Mirrovr of Monsters* [London: T. H., 1587], F1$^{v}$). From there Hotson, upholding the orthodox position on *Groat's-worth*, constructed a convoluted argument attempting to show that Greene was making a charge of duplicity, not cruelty. This succeeds in missing the obvious point that the tiger's duplicity functions in the service of his cruelty.

**Page 38** *"He is a great wheeler-dealer," "After the death scene"*: Homer D. Swander, "The Rediscovery of *Henry VI*," *Shakespeare Quarterly*, 29 (1978): 155, 156.

*"The scene"*: Briley, "Edward Alleyn," p. 330.

*"Greene was not"*: Muriel C. Bradbrook, "Beasts and Gods: Greene's *Groats-worth of Witte* and the Social Purpose of *Venus and Adonis*," *Shakespeare Survey 15* (Cambridge: Cambridge University Press, 1962), p. 65.

*A summer Shakespeare festival*: Held at Antioch College in Yellow Springs, Ohio, in 1981.

**Page 39** *"Bene played"*: *A Knack to Know a Knave* (London: Richard Jones, 1594). The title page also included this notation: "*VVith KEMPS applauded Merrimentes* of the men of Goteham, in receiuing the King into Goteham."

*Henslowe responded*: *Henslowe Papers*, ed. Greg, p. 40.

**Page 40** *"Enter a region"*: Chambers, *Stage*, 2: 129.

*"Probably some play-books"*: Chambers, *Shakespeare*, 1:49-50.

*"Strongly supports"*: Mary Edmond, "Pembroke's Men," *Review of English Studies*, n.s., 25 (1974): 130. Simon Jewell, the testator, made bequests to a number of his fellow actors. Edmond comments, "The fact that Shakespeare is not mentioned in the will suggests that he was not...one of Pembroke's Men."

**Page 41** *Alleyn's roles*: For a summary of the available evidence see Chambers, *Stage*, 2:297-98, and Edwin Nungezer, *A Dictionary of Actors and of Other Persons Associated with the Public Representation of Plays in England Before 1642* (New Haven: Yale University Press, 1929), pp. 7-8.

**Page 42** *"The adaptation," "I believe"*: *The Wars of the Roses, Adapted for the Royal Shakespeare Company from William Shakespeare's* Henry VI, Parts I, II, III *and* Richard III, adapted by John Barton in collaboration with Peter Hall (London: British Broadcasting Corp., 1970), pp. xxiii, xxiv. Hall commented that the "case for adaptation is based on my conviction that the plays do not work in unadapted form. I have seen the original version played twice and found it as often a mess of angry and undifferentiated barons, thrashing about in a mass of diffuse narrative" (p. vii). At least some Elizabethans would have agreed: in the prologue to *Every Man in His Humour* (1599) Ben Jonson promised the audience that they would not be forced to listen to "York and Lancaster's long jars." Yet Andrew Cairncross, a leading textual critic, has declared that "the main positive general argument for Shakespeare's complete authorship" is "that of unity of conception and execution....The planning of *3 Henry VI,* and its thorough integration with *1* and *2 Henry VI* and with *Richard III,* are the surest guarantees of Shakespearean authorship" (*The Third Part of King Henry VI*, ed. Andrew S. Cairncross, The [New] Arden Shakespeare [London: Methuen, 1964], p. xliii). It would seem that brilliance in organization exists in the eye of the beholder.

Fourteen years after Hall's production the Royal Shakespeare Company offered the three parts of *Henry VI* in full, and the consensus that emerged this time was that the plays were Shakespeare's work—and moreover, they weren't such bad work as all that. Indeed, in an article for *Shakespeare Quarterly* Homer Swander offered the view that "no acting company since the death of Shakespeare has performed a greater service to its art." Unlike Hall, who had seen two *Henry VIs* and found them two too many, Swander deplored the dearth of offerings: "We need still more productions, of course, literally hundreds of them."

On the authorship issue Swander indicated that a conversation with the actress who played Queen Margaret "silenced the question forever for me." She assured him that the revisionist "arguments are ridiculous to anyone who has been inside the scripts by playing them. There is a feeling in the playing that only Shakespeare can give. All those others, even Marlowe and Jonson, are shit, pure shit, alongside him. And that pure Shakespearean quality is in these plays" (Swander, "Rediscovery," pp. 146, 147, 152).

*"Many scholars"*: Taylor, "Canon," p. 112.

**Page 43** *"The 'tiger's heart'"*: S. Schoenbaum, *Shakespeare: The Globe and the World* (New York: Oxford University Press, 1979), p. 60.

*On the* Henry VI *authorship issue*: The first edition of *Richard Duke of York* was printed as an octavo—eight pages to a signature—rather than the more typical format of quarto for an issue of a single play. Neither it nor the second edition, which came out in 1600, bore any indication of authorship, a situation not uncommon at the time. Shakespeare's name was not linked with the play until 1619—three years after his death—when Thomas Pavier brought out a combined edition that included *The First Part of the Contention,* the play that later became *2 Henry VI.* Yet the evidence here is equivocal: Pavier claimed he was publishing an enlarged edition when he was not, and in the same series of plays he erroneously attributed *A Yorkshire Tragedy* to Shakespeare. In addition, Pavier falsified dates on the title pages of some of the authentic Shakespeare plays that he published. For an interesting account of the sorting out of the Pavier editions see Alfred W. Pollard, *Shakespeare Folios and Quartos: A Study in the Bibliography of Shakespeare's Plays, 1594-1685* (orig. ed., 1909; reprint ed., New York: Cooper Square Publishers, 1970). In the First Folio of 1623 a revised and much superior text of *Richard Duke of York* was published as *3 Henry VI.*

Yet for all of its flaws, the octavo does have its uses. At several points it remains closer to the source material, which is what one would expect from a text that is not itself the earliest version but which is an imperfect reflection of that version. As an example, the stage direction at 2.6 reads in the octavo, "Enter *Clifford* wounded, with an arrow in his necke." That follows the account in Hall's chronicle, but the Folio eliminates the detail of the placement of the arrow. Hall mentioned secret conferences that Richard held with his brothers, and the octavo reflects these with a whispered parley between Richard and George at 5.1.82, a piece of stage business that the Folio deletes. Interestingly, the octavo contains the earliest recorded example of "Et tu, Brute?" It was not retained in the Folio text, but the reviser was able to put it to good use elsewhere.

The darkening of Richard's character in the Folio is particularly intriguing. The most significant occasion comes at the point where George deserts his two brothers to join the Lancastrians. Edward, who has upheld the family's claim on the throne following the death of their father, asks Richard—then Duke of Gloucester and later Richard III—whether he will remain loyal. Richard responds:

> *I* my Lord, in despight of all that shall
> Withstand you. For why hath Nature
> Made me halt downe right, but that I
> Should be valiant and stand to it, for if
> I would, *I* cannot runne awaie.

(*The true Tragedie of Richard Duke of Yorke, and the death of good King Henrie the Sixt* [London: Thomas Millington, 1595], D4$^{v}$-D5$^{r}$. I have retained the lineation of the octavo.) This Richard is nearly likable, not so different from a fat man who jests of his girth. The last part of the speech, though, is not to be found in the Folio.

Alexander ruled that this "instance does not justify a revision theory. Good texts have occasional lapses" (*Shakespeare's* Henry VI, p. 114). Whatever might be said about textual theory, the equivalent text in the Folio clearly reveals the reality of revision. The author of *Richard III* had to find a way to make Richard the greater malefactor in standing by his brother, and Shakespeare deftly accomplished that task through an aside spoken by Richard. It comes in response to an invitation by George to join him and leave Edward:

> Not I: my thoughts aim at a further matter;
> I stay not for the love of Edward, but the crown.

(*3 Henry VI*, 4.1.123-24.) In just two lines Shakespeare has given us the Richard we love to hate.

**Page 44** *"Most studio executives"*: Edgar J. Scherick, review of *Reel Power: The Struggle for Influence and Success in the New Hollywood*, by Mark Litwak, *American Film*, January/February, 1987, p. 71.

*"It is evident"*: A. D. Wraight, *In Search of Christopher Marlowe: A*

*Pictorial Biography* (London: Macdonald, 1965), p. 306. Wraight based her view of the authorship of *1 Henry VI* on a study done in the 1920s by Allison Gaw. Gaw had assigned scenes in the play to four writers—Marlowe, Peele, possibly Greene, and an unnamed playwright. Wraight chose to put forth Alleyn as the fourth playwright; and to account for Greene's rancor toward him, she pointed to the pressures of the play's "hasty composition for the opening of the Rose theatre" (p. 203). However, Alleyn's 1592 season at the Rose began with a revival of Greene's *Friar Bacon and Friar Bungay.* It was nearly two weeks before the performance of the play that Henslowe recorded in his *Diary* as *harey the vj*. Most commentators have been inclined to accept this as an early version of *1 Henry VI*; and Henslowe's inscription "ne" next to the March 3 entry for *harey the vj* has generally been taken to mean that it was a new play. In that case Gaw would have been correct in noting that it was "the first new play presented in the rebuilt house" (Allison Gaw, *The Origin and Development of* 1 Henry VI *in Relation to Shakespeare, Marlowe, Peele, and Greene*, University of Southern California Studies, First Series, No. 1 [Los Angeles: University of Southern California, 1926], p. 54). Winifred Frazer has offered a radically different interpretation of "ne," suggesting that it denoted a play performed at the Newington Butts playhouse ("Henslowe's 'Ne,'" *Notes and Queries*, n.s., 38 [1991]: 34-35).

Gaw had written tellingly on the theatricality of the "tiger's heart" line, noting that "the line is almost always referred to by critics as simply 'a line that occurs in the *True Tragedy*' or 'in *3 Henry VI*.' But this is an understatement, born of our habit of considering these plays from the standpoint of the study rather than of the theatre. It is really the opening line of the climactic accusation in perhaps the most powerful speech of invective that had, up to that time, ever been heard upon the English stage." Gaw, though, was unconcerned with challenging orthodoxy on the identity of the upstart crow and decided that "Greene was simply applying to the upstart Shakespeare one of the most scorching lines that he had ever heard" (*Origin*, pp. 75, 76). Wraight made no attempt to explain how the "tiger's heart" line belonged to the upstart crow. She regarded it as merely "a line from a scene in a play well-known to theatregoers at the time which would have all the overtones of emotion he [Greene] wished to communicate" (*In Search of*, p. 196).

Wraight commented that "Greene was probably already a sick man" at the time of his collaboration with Alleyn (p. 208), but the evidence on Greene's illness exists in detailed form and indicates that Greene was suffering from poor health for about a month before he died. (See the account included with *The Repentance of Robert Greene*, ed. Harrison, pp. 31-32.) If this evidence is to be trusted, the onset of his illness can then be placed near the beginning of August.

While Wraight viewed "shake-scene" as being "synonymous with a great actor's rant—to 'shake a stage' with passion," she failed to include contemporary references to "stalking Tamburlaine" or mention the incident when the Theatre "cracked." She also overlooked the controversy with *Orlando Furioso* and showed considerable confusion over Will Kemp's use of the word "shakerags," stating that the term was directed at his colleagues when in fact it was aimed at ballad writers. She commented of a woodcut depicting Kemp dancing a morris, "Perhaps his clothes could be called 'shakerags'" (*In Search of*, pp. 197, 207, 210 caption). Hardly: the streamers on Kemp's sleeves are part of the ordinary attire of a morris dancer.

As far as I have been able to determine, the first presentation of the Alleynian position was made by C. A. C. Davis in a letter to the editor of the *Times Literary Supplement* ("The Upstart Crow," August 17, 1951, p. 517). Davis thought that Greene's anger stemmed from his frustration in attempting to create material suitable for the commercial theatre. He viewed Alleyn's acting style as being more "suited to the new verse form of violent passions popularized by Kyd and Marlowe" than "to the bread and margarine prose idylls in which Greene excelled." Davis could have presented a stronger argument had he cited the preface to *Perimedes the Blacksmith* (1588) where Greene wrote of having been satirized "for that I could not make my verses iet vpon the stage in tragicall buskins, euerie worde filling the mouth like the faburden of Bo-Bell, daring God out of heauen with that Atheist *Tamburlan*" (*Greene*, ed. Grosart, 7:7-8). Yet any playwright can experience failure, and that comment was made four years prior to *Groat's-worth.* Greene's success at finding two buyers for *Orlando Furioso* demonstrates that, whatever difficulties he may have encountered in the commercial theatre, being able to sell his work was not among them.

An Alleynian view of *Groat's-worth* was also set forth by Hugh Ross Williamson in his 1972 biographical novel of Marlowe, *Kind Kit.* Ross Williamson noted that in writing an earlier book about Shakespeare he treated the orthodox position on *Groat's-worth* as "a 'source' which one accepts without question." What made the difference for him was approaching "the story from the point of view of Marlowe." In commenting that the "tiger's heart" line "opened one of Alleyn's most memorable speeches in the popular *True Tragedy of Richard Duke of York,*" Ross Williamson cleared up one point but added a fresh bit of confusion. The line does not open the speech, although a hasty reading of Gaw may have left that impression. Ross Williamson was of the belief that the orthodox identification of the upstart crow had undergone "demolition" at the hands of C. F. Tucker Brooke in his 1912 study *The Authorship of 2 and 3 Henry VI* and of Gaw in 1926, yet neither of those writers had attempted the task. He otherwise declared himself unwilling to start to start the revolution, commenting that the identification of Shakespeare as the upstart crow "is the conventional Eng. Lit. theory, accepted by generation after generation of writers, repeated in every textbook and encyclopaedia and too firmly embedded in Shakespearian criticism to be popularly dislodged" (*Kind Kit: An Informal Biography of Christopher Marlowe* [London: Michael Joseph, 1972], p. 256).

**Page 45** *Alleyn as musician*: *Henslowe's Diary*, ed. Walter W. Greg, 2 vols. (London: A. H. Bullen, 1907-08), 2: 9.

*"Greene's 'Tyger's hart'"*: E. A. J. Honigmann, *Shakespeare's Impact on His Contemporaries* (Totowa, N.J.: Barnes & Noble Books), pp. 7-8. Apart from being one of three payees for a 1594 performance at court, Shakespeare did not handle the finances for any company that he belonged to. John Heminges, a co-editor of the First Folio, served most often as payee for court performances by the Lord Chamberlain's men, but even that role would not place Heminges in a position equivalent to Henslowe. See the listing of accounts in Chambers, *Stage*, 4: 164-83.

**Page 46** *"Jack-of-all-trades"*: Ivor Brown, *Shakespeare in His Time* (Edinburgh: Thomas Nelson and Sons, 1960), p. 170. *"The* Johannes factotum": Anthony Burgess, *Shakespeare* (New York: Alfred A. Knopf, 1970), p. 109. *"Shakespeare for Greene"*: Hanspeter Born, *The Rare Wit and the Rude Groom: The Authorship of* A Knack to Know a Knave *in Relation to Greene, Nashe & Shakespeare*, Swiss Studies in English (Bern: Francke Verlag, 1971), p. 159.

*"Plays are of many kinds"*: Dover Wilson, *Essential*, p. 47.

*"William Shakespeare"*: Rowse, *Shakespeare the Man*, p. 40. The function of "producer" did not exist at this time apart from that of actor-manager, a position that Shakespeare did not occupy for his company.

**Page 47** *Four of his establishments*: Sheila Hodges, *God's Gift: A Living History of Dulwich College* (London: Heinemann Educational Books, 1981), p. 12.

**Page 48** *"Hath sondrye tymes"*: Chambers, *Stage*, 4:328. *"To give"*: *Henslowe Papers*, p. 50.

*"With excellent Action"*: Nungezer, *Dictionary*, p. 6. The comment was made by Thomas Dekker.

*"To fetch secretly," "Whereupon the King"*: John Stow, *Annales, or, A Generall Chronicle of England*, updated by Edmund Howes (London: Richard Meighen, 1631), pp. 835, 836.

**Page 49** *"Was this"*: *Dr. Faustus*, 5.1.99-105.

**Page 50** *"£1,000 more"*: Hodges, *God's Gift*, p. 3.

*"Of my blood"*: Ibid., p. 7. *A long succession*: For a complete list see Thomas Lane Ormiston, *Dulwich College Register, 1619 to 1926* (London: J. J. Keliker, 1926), pp. 9-11.

**Page 51** *"This combination"*: Hodges, *God's Gift*, p. 13.

**Page 52** *"In his," "Thys clerke," "A drunkard does"*: *OED*, s.v. "conceit," def. 4c. *"Means"*: Hazelton Spencer, *The Art and Life of William Shakespeare* (New York: Harcourt, Brace, 1940), p. 19. *"One who"*: Honigmann, *Impact*, p. 5.

*"The only one"*: *OED*, s.v. "only."

*On "in a country"*: See the note in *Nashe*, ed. McKerrow, 4:192.

**Page 53** *"Greene's interest"*: James S. Dean, Jr., "Antedatings from Robert Greene," *Notes and Queries*, n.s., 16(1969): 126. *"The ends"*: *Epicoene, or The Silent Woman*, 2d Prologue, 1-2.

*"The Elizabethan actor"*: Glynne Wickham, "The Stage and Its Surroundings," in *The Third Globe: Symposium for the Reconstruction of the Globe Playhouse, Wayne State University, 1979*, ed. C. Walter Hodges, S. Schoenbaum, and Leonard Leone (Detroit: Wayne State University Press, 1981), p. 137. *"Stalking Tamburlaine"*: See A. J. Gurr, "Who Strutted and Bellowed?" *Shakespeare Survey 16* (Cambridge: Cambridge University Press, 1963), pp. 98-101. *"Dost stampe"*: *The Dramatic Works of Thomas Dekker*, ed. Fredson Bowers, 4 vols. (Cambridge: Cambridge University Press, 1953-61), 1:364. The attack was specifically aimed at Ben Jonson, who had served an apprenticeship as a bricklayer.

*"The* Tamerlanes*"*: *Ben Jonson*, ed. C. H. Herford and Percy and Evelyn Simpson, 11 vols. (Oxford: Clarendon Press, 1925-52), 8:587. In a laudatory epigram "To Edward Alleyn" Jonson wrote that "others speake, but onely thou dost act" (8:57). This strikes a note similar to a statement from Thomas Nashe: "Not *Roscius* nor *Æsope* [an actor, not the writer of fables], those admyred tragedians that haue liued euer since before Christ was borne, could euer performe more in action than famous *Ned Allen*" (*Nashe*, ed. McKerrow, 1:215). For a comment by Dekker see my notes to page 48. In assessing Alleyn's reputation among his contemporaries Gurr noted that "when Jonson wrote his praise, the word 'act' still had a residual connotation of the use of (rhetorical) 'Action,' and it cannot be insignificant that Jonson joined Nashe and Dekker in applying the term to Alleyn" ("Who Strutted," p. 97).

**Page 54** "Allens Cutlacks *gate"*: Everard Guilpin, *Skialetheia or A Shadowe of Truth, in Certaine Epigrams and Satyres*, ed. D. Allen Carroll (Chapel Hill, N.C.: University of North Carolina Press, 1974), p. 50. *"Vp and downe"*: Gurr, "Who Strutted," p. 98.

*"To cause (a structure)"*: *OED*, s.v. "shake," def. 10. *"Villainous"*:

T[homas] M[iddleton], *The Blacke Booke* (London: Jeffrey Chorlton, 1604), B3^v^, B4^r^.

*"Our nearest approach"*: Chambers, *Stage*, 3:72. *"When* Faustus": *Studies in English Faust Literature: I. The English Wagner Book of 1594*, ed. Alfred E. Richards (Berlin: Verlag von Emil Felber, 1907), p. 75.

**Page 55** *"To life againe"*: *The First Folio of Shakespeare*, The Norton Facsimile, ed. Charlton Hinman (New York: W. W. Norton, 1968), p. 9.

**Page 56** *"And he wrote," the banana story*: Romain Gary, interviewed by François Bondy, *La nuit sera calme* (Paris: Editions Gallimard, 1974), p. 197. Original text of the quotation: "Et il écrivait comme un cochon, comme un vrai cochon, c'était incroyable, ce qui sortait de sa plume." *"He knows"*: Mel Gussow, *Don't Say Yes Until I Finish Talking: A Biography of Darryl F. Zanuck* (Garden City, N.Y.: Doubleday, 1971), p. 206.

*"The punning reference"*: S. Schoenbaum, "The Life of Shakespeare," in Kenneth Muir and S. Schoenbaum, eds., *A New Companion to Shakespeare Studies* (Cambridge: Cambridge University Press, 1971), p. 5. *"A derogatory pun"*: Roland Mushat Frye, *Shakespeare: The Art of the Dramatist* (Boston: Houghton Mifflin, 1970), p. 7.

**Page 57** *"We can argue"*: Alfred Harbage, *Shakespeare without Words and Other Essays* (Cambridge: Harvard University Press, 1972), pp. 98-99n.

*"A ranting actor," "The Poets"*: *OED*, s.v. "tear-throat."

**Page 58** *T. W. Baldwin saw*: *William Shakspere's Small Latine & Lesse Greeke*, 2 vols. (Urbana, Ill.: University of Illinois Press, 1944), 2:666. *"A speculative" and other quotations*: Sigurd Burckhardt, *Shakespearean Meanings* (Princeton, N.J.: Princeton University Press, 1968), pp. 55, 56, 57, 93.

**Page 59** *Black Will and Shakebag* are in *Arden of Faversham*, a play based on an actual crime. *King John* contains a similar expression: John tells the Bastard to "shake the bags/Of hoarding abbots" (3.2.17-18). Peter Levi has offered the comment that *Arden of Faversham* "seems to me to satirize Shakespeare personally." Levi is impressed by the presence of a character named Greene and by Shakebag's seeking refuge with a widow in Southwark. Shakebag cuts her throat and dumps the body in the Thames. He is eventually murdered in the area, while Black Will's fate is to be burned on a stage. In Levi's view "the allusions to Shakespeare in this play are irresistibly funny and convincing, at least as much so as many more famous allusions to him" (*The Life and Times of William Shakespeare* [New York: Henry Holt, 1988], pp. 61, 62).

*"Shakerags"*: *Nine Daies Wonder*, ed. Harrison, p. 29. See the entry in the *OED.*

*"Commentators"*: "Shakespeare the Shake-scene," *Notes and Queries*, n.s., 26(1979): 115.

**Page 60** *"Shakespeare's first venture"*: Bradbrook, "Beasts and Gods," pp. 62, 71. Peter Alexander has commented, "That it was the attack on Shakespeare's honesty contained in Greene's epilogue to his *Groatsworth of Wit* that suggested the publication of such a work as *Venus and Adonis* is a probability not to be overlooked" (*Shakespeare's Life and Art* [London: James Nisbet and Co., 1939], p. 93).

**Page 61** *"*O'er-greene *is surely"*: Edgar I. Fripp, *Shakespeare, Man and Artist,* 2 vols. (London: Oxford University Press, 1938), 1:311. *"Though not much"*: John Berryman, *The Freedom of the Poet* (New York: Farrar, Straus, Giroux, 1976), p. 36. Ellipses in the original.

*"Comparable to"*: *Shakespeare's Sonnets,* ed. Stephen Booth (New Haven: Yale University Press, 1977), p. 362.

**Page 62** *"For they bene"*: *Shepherds Calendar,* "September," 130, 136-39.

**Page 63** *"Gabriel Harvey's"*: *Love's Labour's Lost,* ed. Richard David, The [New] Arden Shakespeare (London: Methuen, 1951), p. 64n. Virginia F. Stern, Harvey's biographer, is more cautious on this point, commenting that Armado is "a character in some but not all respects suggestive of Harvey" (*Gabriel Harvey: His Life, Marginalia and Library* [Oxford: Clarendon Press, 1979], p. 145n.). *"My tender juvenal"*: 1.2.7-8. *"Moth, therefore"*: *LLL,* ed. David, p. xxxvi.

*"Excellently parodied," "is rather"*: *Love's Labour's Lost,* ed. Sir Arthur Quiller-Couch and John Dover Wilson, 2d ed. (Cambridge: Cambridge University Press, 1962), pp. xxxix, xiv. Charles Nicholl, a recent biographer of Nashe, notes that the caricature of Nashe "is, unlike some others in the play, a totally affable sketch" (*Cup of News*, p. 213).

Robert Giroux has suggested that the play "is in some way connected with Greene's savaging of Shakespeare....Our poet's need to prove himself capable of a learned comedy (since the thrust of Greene's slur was against his lack of a university education) would have been great. It is no accident that the play has so much rhyme and so little blank verse. Greene's taunt '[he] supposes he is as well able to bombast out a blank verse as the best of you' apparently hit its mark" (*The Book Known as Q: A Consideration of Shakespeare's Sonnets* [New York: Atheneum, 1982], pp. 135, 137). Yet in avoiding the use of blank verse Shakespeare would be proving his enemy right even as he was failing to respond to him in any recognizable way.

**Page 64** *"Green indeed"*: *LLL*, 1.2.81. *"There may"*: ed. David, p. 22n. *"My penny"*: 3.1.25. *"The similar expression"*: ed. David, p. 45n.

*"The penny is"*: The proverb was first recorded by William Camden in 1605, a decade or so after *Love's Labour's Lost* was first performed, but presumably it was in use before finding its way into print.

*"The thrice three Muses"*: *A Midsummer Night's Dream*, 5.1.52-55. *"There is nothing"*: *The Works of William Shakespeare*, ed. James O. Halliwell, 16 vols. [London: privately published, 1853-65], 5:6. Halliwell was later Halliwell-Phillipps. *"This is fairly clearly"*: A. L. Rowse, *Shakespeare's Globe: His Intellectual and Moral Outlook* (London: Weidenfeld & Nicolson, 1981), p. 25.

**Page 65** *"These coincidences"*: *As You Like It*, ed. Sir Arthur Quiller-Couch and John Dover Wilson (Cambridge: Cambridge University Press, 1926), p. 134. Agnes Latham in the New Arden edition argues that "the parallels are less striking when they are seen as poetical commonplaces," and points out that "both Shakespeare and Greene owe the name Orlando to Ariosto" ([London: Methuen, 1975], pp. xxxi, xxxii). Yet Shakespeare chose to change the character's name from Rosader to Orlando, and the love poems hanging from trees constitute a distinctive stage device. *"Tedious homily"*: 3.2.152, 216-20.

*"To the celestial"*: *Hamlet*, 2.2.109-11.

**Page 66** *"Notable"*: Bradbrook, *Poet in His World*, p. 50. *"Possibly as a gloss"*: G. M. Pinciss, "Shakespeare, Her Majesty's Players and Pembroke's Men," *Shakespeare Survey 27* (Cambridge: Cambridge University Press, 1974), p. 130.

*"To the Most Honored"*: *Nashe*, ed. McKerrow, 2:9. *"Forbid us"*: *Hamlet*, ed. Harold Jenkins, The [New] Arden Shakespeare (London: Methuen, 1982), p. 463.

*"We are"*: Fitzroy Pyle, *The Winter's Tale: A Commentary on the Structure* (London: Routledge & Kegan Paul, 1969), p. x.

**Page 67** *The name Mamillius*: This was noted as a possibility by Geoffrey Bullough in *Narrative and Dramatic Sources of Shakespeare*, 8 vols. (London: Routledge & Kegan Paul; New York: Columbia University Press, 1957-75), 8:124. *The coast of Bohemia*: "The Mariners descryed the coast of *Bohemia*" (*Greene*, ed. Grosart, 4:302). *"It is curious"*: Kenneth Muir, *Shakespeare's Sources, 1: Comedies and Tragedies* (London: Methuen, 1957), p. 249.

*"Shakespeare seems"*: *The Winter's Tale*, ed. Baldwin Maxwell, The Pelican Shakespeare (Baltimore, Md.: Penguin Books, 1956), p. 16.

**Page 69** *An old joke*: This was recorded by Ben Hayes. I have claimed the joketeller's prerogative and made a few small changes. See *The Ben Hayes Scrapbook*, ed. Jay Hoster and Christine Hayes (Columbus, Ohio: Ravine Books, 1991), p. 71.

# Index